BEN KATCHOR

FREDERICK LUIS ALDAMA, SERIES EDITOR

BEN
KATCHOR

BENJAMIN FRASER

UNIVERSITY PRESS OF MISSISSIPPI / JACKSON

The University Press of Mississippi is the scholarly publishing agency of
the Mississippi Institutions of Higher Learning: Alcorn State University,
Delta State University, Jackson State University, Mississippi State University,
Mississippi University for Women, Mississippi Valley State University,
University of Mississippi, and University of Southern Mississippi.

www.upress.state.ms.us

Title page portrait by Antony Hare

The University Press of Mississippi is a member
of the Association of University Presses.

First printing 2023

∞

Library of Congress Cataloging-in-Publication Data

Names: Fraser, Benjamin, author.
Title: Ben Katchor / Benjamin Fraser.
Other titles: Biographix.
Description: Jackson : University Press of Mississippi, 2023. | Series:
Biographix | Includes bibliographical references and index.
Identifiers: LCCN 2023017547 (print) | LCCN 2023017548 (ebook) | ISBN
9781496848529 (hardcover) | ISBN 9781496848512 (trade paperback) | ISBN
9781496848505 (epub) | ISBN 9781496848499 (epub) | ISBN 9781496848482
(pdf) | ISBN 9781496848475 (pdf)
Subjects: LCSH: Katchor, Ben—Criticism and interpretation. |
Cartoonists—United States. | Comic books, strips, etc.—United States.
| Urban landscape architecture—Comic books, strips, etc. | New York
(N.Y.)—Comic books, strips, etc.
Classification: LCC PN6727.K28 Z65 2023 (print) | LCC PN6727.K28 (ebook)
| DDC 741.5/69—dc23/eng/20230815
LC record available at https://lccn.loc.gov/2023017547
LC ebook record available at https://lccn.loc.gov/2023017548

British Library Cataloging-in-Publication Data available

CONTENTS

PREFACE

Why did I jump at the chance to write this volume on Ben Katchor's comics? I don't believe I had ever heard of him until I read a brief essay by Mark Feldman titled "The Urban Studies of Ben Katchor." I was interested in urban comics, and one lucky day I stumbled upon Drawn & Quarterly's twenty-fifth anniversary edition of Katchor's *Cheap Novelties: The Pleasures of Urban Decay*. I was stunned. It was like nothing I had seen before. While writing about *Cheap Novelties* as part of chapter 4 of my book *Visible Cities, Global Comics* (2019), I knew very well that I was late to the party.

Delving further into Katchor's published text and image works since then has confirmed that fact for me. Here was an artist who received a MacArthur Fellowship in 2000, and whose comics, drawn from the New York experience, had already saturated the city's environment—or certain cultural corners of it at least. His earlier work was highly visible in the pages of the *Village Voice*, *New York Press*, and *The Forward / Jewish Daily Forward*—not to mention in the display windows of a kosher restaurant on the Lower East Side. More on that later in the book.

His comics have also had quite an impact beyond print and beyond New York City. I was pleased to rediscover that two panels by the artist had been included in the artwork accompanying R.E.M.'s album *Out of Time* (1991). Katchor recently clarified for me that these were original drawings commissioned by Michael Stipe, who had been shown Katchor's comics by a mutual friend. More recently, the artist has drawn from his famous character Julius Knipl for what he has called a cartoon radio show. He has developed several musical theater collaborations with Mark Mulcahy, among other projects (see his website, katchor.com). As guest editor for Houghton Mifflin Harcourt's *Best American Comics 2017* showcase, Katchor delivered on his commitment to promoting innovation in comics. If you have never heard of him, then, like me, you must not have been paying enough attention.

What most excites me about Katchor's comics is something that Theodor Adorno, in *Aesthetic Theory*, called the enigmatic character of art. Let me explain. Throughout the 1900s, the comic had hardly been known for being enigmatic in the wider social imagination. For much of this recent history, the art form's reputation depended on the popular press and on associations with the mass market for children. With the rise of underground and alternative comics, not to mention the contemporary rebranding of the graphic novel, comics continued to connote accessibility even as they grew in prestige during the latter part of the twentieth century. But Katchor's comics are decidedly enigmatic. Some might find them difficult.

Readers of Katchor's comics who expect to encounter the regularized beats of the newspaper strip, the in-your-face countercultural critique of the underground, or the hallmark introspection of autobiographical comics will surely come away confused. Taken as a whole, the artist's strips and pages are perplexing. Derek Parker Royal and Andy Kunka's podcast interview with Katchor (*Comics Alternative Podcast*, March 13, 2013) cited a panel from *Hand-Drying in America* whose text functions equally well as a characterization of the artist's work. It mentions "a deluxe full-color edition of an esoteric literary comic strip" (minute 25; this panel appears on the inside back cover of *HDA*). So let's add esoteric and literary to our list. We are dealing with a creator who deals in philosophical quandaries, offers social commentary, and refuses to be limited by trends tied to the current moment. His is a broad view of social life, informed by history, and conditioned by time's ebb and flow. In his own words: "I think about all of time at every moment" (Katchor, on *Comics Alternative Podcast*, minute 36).

Ben Katchor's enigmatic aesthetics are also, in the very sense that Adorno intended, bound up with history and social consciousness. This is true in more than one way.

While he would seemingly reject the label of a Jewish comics artist in the religious or dogmatic sense, Katchor is quite at home evoking Yiddish-speaking neighborhoods of a certain era in New York's history, depicting the persistence of eastern European / Ashkenazic food culture, and even dramatizing a fictionalized tale of Jewish life in colonial America. Neither are references to the Pentateuch, the Talmud, Kabbalah, Passover, and Chanukah infrequent across his works. The first strip included in his collection *Julius Knipl, Real Estate Photographer* even includes a reference to the kabbalistic concept of *tsimtsum* (see chap. 2).

Working-class struggles echo in the strips that focus on labor, manufacturing, distribution, and consumption. As Marx put it, modern laborers are alienated from the product of their labor, from each other, and from themselves. Katchor responds to this set of social conditions by using his comics as a potential disalienation. The artist likes looking behind the curtain, so to speak, to illustrate how the market economy really functions, which is most frequently to disempower and to dehumanize. Still, his comics appeal to our sense that we are not merely the products of a large social machine.

There are also the questions his comics pose regarding the social nature of wealth, the veneer of privilege and entitlement, and the vacuousness of spectacle. These interrogations play out in an urban context focused on travel, leisure time, authentic culture, and capitalistic development. Here the city is produced by speculators, developers and capitalists who are interested in its potential exchange value, rather than the use value it might have for its inhabitants.

In short, the urban experience is essential for understanding Ben Katchor's comics. On this larger urban frame, Katchor hangs a number of his other concerns—as above, the market economy, food culture, and travel/leisure, but also material culture, print culture, rural spaces, the natural world, and much more.

Here I should admit a certain professional bias. As a scholar of the urban environment, and as founding editor of the *Journal of Urban Cultural Studies*, I approach Katchor's largely urban comics using what I have elsewhere elaborated as an urban cultural studies method. Adapted from Raymond Williams's formulation, this approach gives equal weight to the urban project and the urban formation, linking the built environment of the modern city with its comics representation. The modern city is both the seat and the product of social power. It has had a great impact on our collective consciousness, as urban thinkers such as Louis Wirth, Robert Park, Georg Simmel, and David Harvey have cataloged. Jane Jacobs and Henri Lefebvre have insisted on cities as complex organisms whose significance is not exhausted by the specialized sciences, respectively. For them, the urban environment is not just a site of power and control but also an incubator of spontaneity, difference, innovation, and even joy. All these contradictory characteristics of cities are rendered visible in Katchor's wonderful comics art.

Though this contribution to the mid-length Biographix series by the University Press of Mississippi is not intended to be totalizing, I have tried to include as many selections of Ben Katchor's work from the late 1980s through 2020 as I could. In each chapter, I seek to balance examination of his prominent themes with close readings of individual comics pages. The latter analyses are particularly important if readers are to gain an appreciation of Katchor's graphic style, his preferred formal features, and his characteristic comics storytelling.

ACKNOWLEDGMENTS

I am grateful to series director Frederick Luis Aldama for supporting this foray into the work of one of my favorite comics artists; thanks also to Lisa McMurtray of the University Press of Mississippi, who is a joy to work with. Ian Gordon's book of interviews was an indispensable reference and an inspiration to boot. Thanks to Abby, Steven, and also to the graduate students in my fall 2022 seminar on comics and graphic novels for discussions surrounding a number of Ben Katchor's comics. I am grateful to Ruth; may *Hand-Drying in America*, which I bought two copies of in Williamsburg, Virginia, continue to bring joy to your many visitors. A shout-out to Mark Feldman, whom I have never met, but whose wonderful essay on Katchor first set me on this course. I thank Ben Katchor himself for providing permission to publish the images contained in this book, as well as for encouraging the cover art selection of "On the Newsstand." I also thank the artist for our discussions over email, which have informed the book. Of course, all errors, simplifications, overemphases, or conclusions remain my own.

It is a minor thing, but as it happened, I was delving into Katchor's comics legacy at the same time that I found myself reading intensely the work of Gershom Scholem, Walter Benjamin, Isaac Bashevis Singer, and Grace Paley, as well as other books linked with the broad themes of Judaic studies, Yiddish literature, and New York. These texts informed my perspective in important ways, even if they are arguably only indirectly relevant to my analyses. For example, the *Jewish New York* (2012) trilogy, whose volumes cover the periods of 1654–1864 (vol. 1, by Rock),

1840–1920 (vol. 2, by Polland and Soyer), and 1920–2010 (vol. 3, by Gurock), seems to me a valuable companion piece for approaching some of Katchor's work, including both the earlier milieu of *The Jew of New York* and the more contemporary urban setting of the Julius Knipl strips. I must mention Rabbi Seltzer and the members of his community class on the Zohar that I attended virtually in fall 2021 and fall 2022—I am so very grateful for being included in discussions on religion, history, and identity that originated in this kabbalistic work from medieval Spain but went far beyond. For me, at least, exploring Katchor's work has been an exercise not strictly unrelated to these specific intellectual pleasures, as will become evident in chapters 2 and 4.

All of this is to say that this project has been valuable to me at a personal and not merely professional level. Katchor's nuanced comments on his secular Jewish American experience—in interviews collected in *Ben Katchor: Conversations*, for example—prompted further reflection on my own secular Jewish American identity, traced through my father's family, thus connecting with larger migrations of Yiddish speakers who moved to New York from eastern Europe in the early twentieth century. Also, it is hard for me not to connect Katchor's fictitious and not quite New York comics stories with trips to visit extended family in Queens, the Bronx, Long Island, and Manhattan that occurred too long ago. And in his purposeful use of Yiddish phrases and Hebrew script on the comics page, I found one more motivation to continue what I understand may be a postvernacular study of Yiddish and Hebrew. I thus dedicate this book to my extended family of New Yorkers, to Bob and Rose, to the memories of Jeff and of Amy—and, more than anyone else, to the memories of my grandma Melvina and grandpa Len; and most of all to my dad Howard and uncle Joel, who I think would have loved this stuff.

COMMON ABBREVIATIONS

BSD   *Julius Knipl, Real Estate Photographer: The Beauty Supply District*

CN   *Cheap Novelties: The Pleasures of Urban Decay*

CV   *The Cardboard Valise*

DR   *The Dairy Restaurant*

H&F   *Hotel & Farm*

HDA   *Hand-Drying in America*

JK   *Julius Knipl, Real Estate Photographer: Stories*

JNY   *The Jew of New York*

BEN KATCHOR

INTRODUCTION

B en Katchor (1951–) was an early contributor to Art Spiegelman and Françoise Mouly's *Raw* magazine, and he holds the honor of being among very few cartoonists who have been awarded a MacArthur Fellowship (2000).[1] The young Katchor took life drawing classes at the Brooklyn Museum Art School; later studied studio art, art history, and literature at Brooklyn College; and also attended New York's School of Visual Arts. When asked about his graphic style, he has stated that it is inspired by Nicolas Poussin, a seventeenth-century painter.[2] Katchor got his start with "self-published fanzines and [two] issue[s] of *Picture-Story Magazine*," as well as comics published in "*Heavy Metal* (the US edition of *Metal Hurlant*) and *Gasm!* (a poor US magazine influenced by *Heavy Metal*)."[3] Unable to make even a "bare living" from comics, for many years he ran a typesetting and graphic design company with two friends.[4] Today Katchor works at the Parsons School of Design, the New School. Owing to his reputation as a relentless chronicler of city life, his comics promise to be of interest to readers across a number of academic fields. Despite his artistic and critical success, a book dedicated to exploring his comics art has not yet appeared. This concise study hopes to change that lamentable situation.

Katchor has produced an impressive comics legacy that spans four decades. *Cheap Novelties: The Pleasures of Urban Decay* (1991), *Julius Knipl, Real Estate Photographer* (1993), and *The Beauty Supply District* (2000) are collections of strips begun in 1988 in the *New York Press* and the *Jewish Daily Forward*. His book *The Jew of New York* (1998), though it originally appeared in serialization in the

English-language *Forward*, can be described as a long-form comics exploration of fictional events surrounding the historical attempt by Mordecai Manuel Noah to establish a Jewish state in New York in the early nineteenth century.[5] *The Cardboard Valise* (2011) collects what Katchor once described as an "imaginary travelogue strip" and showcases the artist's unique ability to depict everyday urban experiences with an introspective, contemplative, and quite philosophical approach.[6] *Hand-Drying in America* (2013) is a collection of oversize, mostly color comics that he published between 1998 and 2012 in the architecture journal *Metropolis*, after being approached by its art director Carl Lehmann-Haupt. The extensive prose that makes up *The Dairy Restaurant* (2020)—Katchor's illustrated foray into culinary matters—reveals his deep interest in archival research and conveys his characteristic sense of humor. The series of strips he created with the titles *Hotel & Farm* and *The Shoehorn Technique* are still awaiting release in collected form.

Born in New York, Katchor has crafted a comics legacy centered on the sights and sounds of life in the big city. The artist's identification as a New Yorker is not casual. His interest in the metropolis goes far beyond mere necessity and routine familiarity. In his words, "I've always lived in a city, with short breaks during the summer, and so most of my thoughts revolve around architecture. Like a scientist, I want to understand urban life on a microscopic level."[7] As he made the shift from hand-drawn comics to the Cintiq digital tool for his composition, architecture remained a prominent feature of his work. His urban street scenes often privilege towering skyscrapers, venerable mixed-use buildings, and photogenic municipal exteriors, as well as the detailed interiors of crowded restaurants, living quarters, and office spaces. Yet there is an anthropological or sociological bent to his urban research that goes beyond the building's surface. In his role as urban scientist, Katchor is well attuned to the complexity and diversity of life in the city. His comics seek to reveal the most curious habits of the urbanite. He wants to understand how such urban creatures think, what they feel, what they read, what they eat, and how they spend their time in general. Why do they get such a thrill out of a brief escalator ride (*JK*, 40)? What do their choices of shower curtain say about them (*CV*, 59)? When they attend an impromptu speaker event, would they rather hear a lecture titled "The Psychogenesis of a Club Sandwich," "Knickknacks in the Post-industrial Age," or "Is Santa Claus a Jew"? (*JK*, 73).

His vocal range as a comics creator extends far and wide. Katchor's themes span the quotidian and the bizarre, and his moods run from the understated to the raucous. Judge for yourself, but my own feeling is that his strong and easily identifiable comics voice is quite often humorous. Attentive readers will find that there is a range, too, even in the types of laughter his strips can evoke. For instance, he has described *Cheap Novelties* as expressing a "fairly dark humor."[8] One of the strips in *The Beauty Supply District* explores the topic of "semi-professional competitive grave digging" ("The Vivifield Brothers," *BSD*, 30–31). I have laughed aloud many times reading the opening pages of *The Dairy Restaurant*, which could easily double as material for a stand-up comedy special: the Garden of Eden is the first restaurant, the serpent is "a lowly waiter who had it in for his boss," and the story of Adam and Eve provides us not only with "the first account of dressing for dinner" but also with "the first recorded instance of a couple splitting a single dish" (*DR*, 13–17).

Readers might encounter a chance gag or two, but more often Katchor's humor lies in a ridiculous concept or an idea carried too far. It is baked into his very approach. Generally speaking, the obtrusive presence of his hallmark third-person narrator functions to heighten the absurdity of the situations presented. In "Misspent Youth Center" (*BSD*, 55–56), for example, he takes aim at humanity's compulsion to recapture the past. While the strip's narrator comments in neutral terms on the center's business space and the long lines of customers who congregate outside it, a character's word balloon explains the premise to readers: "All the things we purchased are long gone—broken or irretrievably lost—but the money itself, which passed through our hands can be relocated by date and serial number." Such humor is never far from tragedy. Nor is it far from pathos, or from the feeling that we are laughing at the very enterprise of being human, rather than at the actions of an invented character. This comic range results in a truly unique cocktail, something that surely contributes to his reputation as a beloved comics artist.

To be sure, Katchor never gives his text and image work over to humor completely. He seems always to be more interested in deep time. Whether urban or biblical, this is a time of which we normally catch only a brief glimpse. It is something much larger than our grandiose dreams or pathetic foibles, than our ephemeral joys or feelings of loss. Pulled out of time's flow and dispatched to the page, the ideas for his strips retain a lingering sense of incompletion. He succeeds in cultivating a space of impermanence. His characters loiter and malinger in a space that is not entirely their own. During their brief stay, they enjoy the status of being what Katchor has called "victims of design." This can be understood in two ways. In terms of comics form, his characters are victims of the architectural structure of the page. They are enclosed by its panels, grid, and gutters, limited by the finite span of pages they inhabit. But we readers are ourselves—just as are his characters—also victims of the modern city in which we dwell: constrained by its architecture, yet tethered to it and shaped by it.

Katchor's depictions of architectural and urban spaces are quite rich. His pages bring the complexity of cities to life not merely by invoking real estate—per his infamous *Julius Knipl, Real Estate Photographer* strips—but also by considering architecture, urbanism, and everyday urban life more broadly. His comics pages consistently deal with hallmark aspects of the modern city as they have been chronicled by numerous thinkers.[9] This goes beyond the purely material to address consciousness itself. One view holds that the urban environment is a sensorial chaos that threatens the individual psyche with overstimulation.[10] From this perspective, the city is quintessentially a place of constant change, of shifting circumstances. It can in fact be defined by difference itself.[11] Do all of us even see the same city? Katchor puts it this way: "There are many New Yorks. A funny thing happens when you live in a city: everyone knows a somewhat different city—different social worlds, experiences, restaurants. The landmarks are the same, but everything else is different."[12]

Most frequently, Katchor's drawn urbanites wander the streets of a crowded, whirling, and dazzling urban environment, experiencing momentary joys and moments of solitude. At times that solitude can be, itself, a type of joy. Other times it is more a profound loneliness. Lonely urbanites yearn for something that will soothe the pain of their solitude. On the streets, public pay phones ring out plaintively for someone to answer ("The Ringing Pay Phone," *BSD*, 18; see chap. 2), a symbol of humanity's deep-seated need for connection. Katchor is interested in how city dwellers deal with living in a densely populated area whose routine and casual encounters suggest—but never fulfill—their need for connection and community. During his solitary wanderings, the character Julius Knipl spends time contemplating the lingering residue or auras of deeply felt human connections. Existing comics scholarship has underscored the importance of themes of nostalgia and memory in Katchor's work. On his pages, however, these are not mere abstract ideas, but instead embodied social responses to the conditions the metropolis creates. Some of the artist's other strips foreground the fraternal and social organizations, the labor relations, and the cultural ties that have historically bonded people together into urban communities. In his comics, manufacturing, commerce, and tourism provide as much division as they do solidarity and connection (see chap. 3).

Many times, Katchor's interest in urban community connects with the specifically Yiddish-speaking origins of some of New York's urbanites. The artist's secular connections to a transnational eastern European Jewish diaspora are on display throughout a number of his works. The very selection of "Knipl" as the last name for his notorious urban real estate photographer character expresses the depth of these felt connections in his comics work.

Boasting a Yiddish origin, the word and concept of the *knipl* are suggestive of seemingly contradictory notions: both joy and sadness, surprise and neglect, persistence as well as time's passing (see chap. 1). In his illustrated book chronicling the rise and fall of the dairy restaurant, Katchor approaches the idea of culinary modernity within a historical perspective. These developments, which boast strong connections with Jewish food culture, can at once be understood in relation to a pan-European context that supported milk-based dining and vegetarianism. A passion for diasporic food culture also finds its way into his other comics texts here and there (see chap. 4).

In my view, these aspects of his work can hardly be separated from one another. The overt emphasis Katchor places on themes of architecture, commerce, manufacturing, and urban spontaneity coexists with a preference for certain aspects of the secular Jewish American experience, perhaps the Yiddish language and eastern European food, most of all. Readers seeking a biographical explanation for the interrelation of these varied themes can easily find one. In an interview, the artist has stated:

> I grew up in the Brooklyn, NY neighborhoods of Bedford-Stuyvesant, Crown Heights and Kensington. These were neighborhoods filled with first and second-generation Jewish immigrants from Eastern Europe, Puerto-Ricans, African Americans and a small population of Chinese. My father came from Warsaw, Poland in the 1920s. He was a Yiddish speaker with strong socialist and communalist political leanings. He was apprenticed to be a tailor as a boy in Poland, ran a small hotel and chicken farm in Upstate New York before I was born and was in the real-estate business during my childhood.[13]

Katchor says he was not "forced to have a religious education," and he has distanced himself from "organized Jewish religion," acknowledging that "I was brought up in the secular, atheist end of Jewish culture."[14] His comments in interviews are critical of nationalisms in general, and he questions the very idea that a monolithic Jewish identity exists or can be consistently traced through history.[15] Katchor has said that "I can only identify with the history of leftist, atheist and internationalist Jewish culture, and that only as history. The only cultural identity I have is being a New Yorker."[16]

Such statements may risk underemphasizing the comics artist's strong connection to Yiddish. As Katchor himself explains, it is "a language connected to a secular Jewish culture whose development was truncated, in part, by WWII."[17] Though he says, "I always spoke English"—that is, not Yiddish—he was nonetheless exposed to the language at a formative time in his childhood.[18] No surprise, then, that Katchor incorporates the Yiddish language and Hebrew script into his comics, or that he once even wrote an entire strip in Yiddish.[19] He has said that he follows Yiddish music.[20] He named the character in his comic-turned-musical *The Slugbearers of Kayrol Island* after "Yiddish author, Alexander Harkavy," and he references Sholem Aleichem, I. L. Peretz, and Isaac Bashevis Singer in *The Dairy Restaurant*.[21] Some may associate the image of this diasporic Yiddish-speaking community with a section of New York City's urban fabric. Not everything has been conserved from Yiddish's lengthy history. As Katchor has said in his interviews: "People think there is a whole body of very early Yiddish literature there is no record of anymore. . . . I'm talking about earlier printed books, and it got lost. Things get lost."[22] Like Yiddish literature, the Yiddish language itself—its place in a diasporic, transnational, eastern European Jewish culture—has had, at times, an uncertain future.[23] Of course, Yiddish today is thriving within certain circles; one just has to know where to look.

To look at Katchor's comics is at once to marvel at his invented world and to be dazzled and disappointed by our own. But merely looking is not enough. I join the comics scholar Ian Hague in his statement that it is crucial to "challenge the idea that comics are a purely visual medium." We must acknowledge that "they are in fact possessed of a wide variety of properties that address themselves to readers' senses of hearing, touch, smell and in some instances taste as well." Katchor's comics are well suited for this sort of multisensory approach, and my response has been to dedicate each chapter of this book to a different sense: sight (chap. 1), hearing (chap. 2), touch (chap. 3), and smell/taste (chap. 4).[24] This approach should make the book you are reading more dynamic than a mere chronological exploration. Katchor's years of conducting research on the urban experience have led him to craft strips that are rich with all manner of sensory details. Whether his drawn comics scenes boast direct or merely implicit connections with the built environment of New York City, they are motivated by the sights, sounds, tactile experiences, smells, tastes, and feelings of life generated in the metropolis. The visual sense is no doubt primary. But vision is not the only sense used by readers who immerse themselves in Katchor's storytelling. Over the course of the book, I draw attention to the richness of Katchor's art by concentrating on the specific aesthetic qualities of his works as they connect with the themes briefly outlined earlier. The result should be an accessible but still urban treatment of his comics art.

The four chapters that follow explore Katchor's comics voice and his varied themes by prioritizing the urban phenomenon as it appears on his comics pages. Thus, word/thought balloons, narrative voice, use of panel and page space, graphic style, color (particularly in more recent work), and other such matters of composition are just as important as the appearance of drawn buildings, architectural details, and solitary figures in his strips—or his themes of time, memory, and urban wandering, for that matter.

There is no better way to begin this book, and close this introduction, than with a brief analysis of two of his early comics. Katchor's hallmark interest in the urban phenomenon is on display in both "Italian Ices" (1988) and "The Corner Location" (1989). While these two examples may not be as well-known as his continuing strips and later collections, they promise a number of advantages. Each is highly innovative in its own way. The first is in many ways a character study. In "Italian Ices," the artist delves deeply into a lone individual's psychology, using a characteristically drifting style of narration complemented by more subjective images. The second is a more ambitious formalist experiment. In "The Corner Location," character development takes a back seat to design issues and architecture, with the narrative highlighting the urban phenomenon as a place of encounters. Together, the strips differ in ways that showcase the impressive breadth of Katchor's formal choices.

The Urban Sensorium

In the four-page comic "Italian Ices" (1988), many of Katchor's hallmark interests are on display. The story can be briefly summarized: prompted by the sound of a metal scoop scraping across ice—or, rather, by the memory of this sound—a man interested in automobile mechanics decides to switch his studies to refrigeration. He follows an Italian ice pushcart around town, seeking to learn more about the business itself. Along the way, his childhood memories come flooding back: of "Bushwick—1956," "Crown Heights—1957," "Flatbush—1958." Perhaps as a rebellion against his bank-manager father, who "begs him not to go into a seasonal business," an obsession overtakes him. At one point, he digs through a trash bag, hoping to find clues that will aid him in his quest. Success! He discovers the sources of certain flavor ingredients and the dry ice needed to keep the pushcarts cool throughout the hot summer days. He tracks down the location of the Ciro Brothers company, and he speaks with one of the owners at a lunch counter across the street. This owner spins him a yarn relating the heavily mythologized origins of the business, which lie in snow sourced from a hidden cave on Mount Etna long ago. Upon listening to the business's origin tale, which mixes geography, history, fantasy, humor, and even violence ("And they killed and took it!"), the protagonist becomes uncomfortable and abruptly excuses himself. The text of the comic's last panel reads: "As the weather becomes cooler so does his passion for Italian ices." With the man's entrepreneurial dreams now deflated, the whole experience becomes yet another fleeting moment of urban life.

"Italian Ices" is a quintessentially urban story. Here, just as in Katchor's Julius Knipl strips, which he first began publishing that same year in *The Forward*, the urban environment is crucial. The toponyms are a dead giveaway that the setting is New York, and Ciro's Wholesale distributing even has a Brooklyn address. Even without these references, however, readers quickly gain a sense of the city's size, density, and complexity. As the protagonist follows the Italian ice man, we see visual references to multimodal transportation: a bus line, a trip on the train, and pedestrian-friendly sidewalks. Everywhere we encounter the hustle and bustle of modern urban life, the cacophony of the streets. The city is a sensorium of both sights and sounds. A passing ambulance, or "noisemaker," draws an apartment dweller to the window. A public works crew digs up a patch of asphalt on a street corner. A man in a bow tie and vest barks a command at the vendor as he stores his pushcart. Someone empties a bucket onto the curb. These seemingly atmospheric sights and sounds are arguably just as important as the plot of the comic. As we will see many times in Katchor's work, the city itself is the story.

Pacing is another crucial element of Katchor's comics storytelling. Here, his use of light and shadow to convey the passing of time is worthy of note. On the third page, day shifts to night and back twice in the span of four rows. This transition occurs precisely after the comic's midpoint, causing readers to feel a corresponding acceleration in the story's action. It represents the culmination of the protagonist's frenzied investigation. Now losing sleep over his obsession, the protagonist drops into a momentary slumber on the train while scouting out the Kelso Corporation's dry ice building in Rumsey, New York. This temporal dilation is a way of expressing the magnitude of the urban environment and the complexity of its decentralized distribution networks. The man's entrepreneurial dream requires that he gain knowledge of urban form, that he understand the large city as a series of interconnected nodes.

The dynamic acceleration of the story's narration is remarkable because it is decidedly at odds with what might be called the hallmark timelessness of the artist's style. As my analyses throughout this book emphasize, Katchor has a penchant for presenting characters, thoughts, and objects as if outside of time. Many times, his strips meander. Other times, they end abruptly or peter out anticlimactically. Readers are likely to get caught up in the details or to fixate on an unusual idea—as his characters do—rather than hew closely to the chains of action and reaction that, in the popular imagination at least, are synonymous with the comics medium. What makes "Italian Ices" so interesting is the way in which the artist combines the nameless main character's visceral propulsion through the streets with the more contemplative mood that tends to predominate in his Julius Knipl strips. If one wants to identify an "action comic" in Katchor's oeuvre, then this might very well be it. Still, the story's action is not pursued to the detriment of Katchor's characteristic indulgences of the protagonist's subjective consciousness.

The comic's first page is at once propulsive in its overall design and contemplative in its content (fig. I.1). Lacking the standard grid pattern that many readers will associate with the comics medium, the page instead boasts a more difficult reading path that traces along the page margins and ends up in the very center. The first two panels at top left are interlocking parallelograms separated by an arrow-shaped gutter. This marked use of panel framing points readers to continue reading to the right. Yet, having followed this visual instruction, one finds that the reading path of the page continues in a vertical descent at the right margin and then crawls right to left at the page bottom, before climbing vertically upward at the left margin and splashing into a central image bearing the comic's title. In this way, the comic's form becomes an expression of the character's inner psychological state. The spiraling form of the reading path mimics the protagonist's own spiraling into mania. In the central title panel, Katchor obscures the man's own thought balloon by placing his body over it, such that the text underneath is not fully visible to the reader—another excessive formal expression of the character's flight of fancy. This subtle formal detail is at once a prompt to the reader and a characterization of the protagonist as a pathetic figure. One thinks of the Yiddish schlemiel: a fool, for lack of a better word.

Despite the propulsive page design, the story panels consistently emphasize the protagonist's inner state over the continuity of his urban travels. That is, very few panel transitions present a cause and effect or convey a match on action. Hardly any visual information is repeated from one panel to the next, with the exception of the image of a chocolate Italian ice at page bottom. This stream-of-consciousness effect is achieved through several unconventional decisions that reveal what might be called Katchor's overarching style. His preferred perspective is that of a fly on the wall: detached, floating, uninvested in any given outcome. His is an observing consciousness that is not entirely objective but sometimes sympathizes with, and other times smirks at, the trials and tribulations of his characters. A certain humor results from this emotional distance, though it tends to be subtle, an added dimension of the comic rather than its main element.

The very syntax of the first page's text is poetic. The first three text boxes are set along the length of the top row of left-to-right panels and read: "To a familiar sound / in a pleated paper shirt / he switches from auto mechanics to refrigeration." These three lines are not connected logically but instead seem to be snatched from a stream of consciousness. When these words are read in connection with the images, their meaning becomes clearer, but the poetic sensibility does not dissipate. The second text box, "in a pleated paper shirt," refers not to the protagonist himself but to the disposable paper cup in which the Italian ice is served to the customer. This text-image combination follows an image of the protagonist wearing a collared shirt and seated in a classroom. Thus, if the fancy paper cup is personified, elevated by wearing a "pleated paper shirt," by consequence the man is correspondingly objectified, reduced to the status of a passive object.

Fig. I.1. Ben Katchor, first page of the four-page "Italian Ices" comic, *Bad News*, no. 3 (1988): 3–6, published by Fantagraphics Books. Reprinted with the generous permission of Ben Katchor.

Fig. I.2. Ben Katchor, second and third pages of "Italian Ices," *Bad News*, no. 3 (1988): 3–6, published by Fantagraphics Books. Reprinted with the generous permission of Ben Katchor.

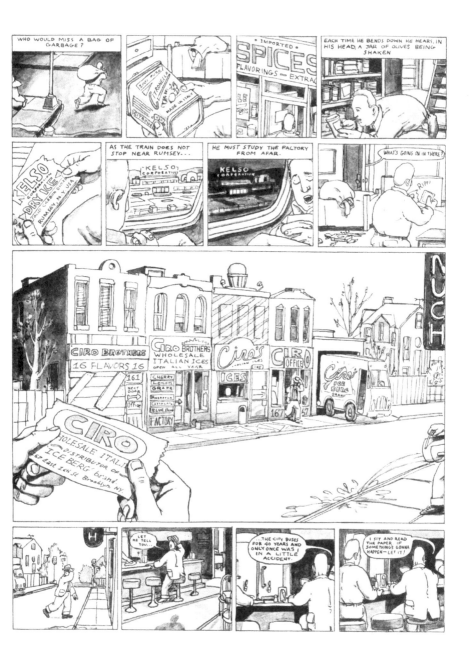

The comic's textual zones are written from the point of view of a third-person narrator, one of the artist's preferred devices. Katchor's narrative voice—here as elsewhere, including the Julius Knipl strips—is dry and detached. It offers matter-of-fact observations but also intrudes on the thoughts of characters. Even so, it can be hesitant to draw conclusions. This narration hovers between expressing sympathy and making an overt judgment on character behavior. In the second page of "Italian Ices," we can see an example of this subtle dance (fig. I.2). Two consecutive panels in the third row read, "He concludes that a secret union exists among these men / And that somehow . . ."; the fact that this thought goes unfinished ("And that somehow . . .") expresses the indeterminacy of Katchor's narration and anticipates the protagonist's lack of commitment, which becomes evident in the comic's finale.

An interesting formal feature of the page can be traced diagonally through three panels starting at the upper left ("A pizza place"), passing down and to the right ("A grocery store"), and ending in the first of these two consecutive panels ("He concludes . . ."). These three panels are rotated counterclockwise just a touch and pulled out from the flat page, as evidenced by a dark shadow line at the left and bottom edges of each one. Hovering above the other panels in the first three rows of the page, which are subjective memories of the past, they form an action sequence in the present. This clear formal distinction between past and present is in direct contrast to the artist's tendency to present temporal disjunction in a relatively unmarked way. So, very often, as in the Ciro origin tale on the last page of "Italian Ices," Katchor shifts from present to past and back without any formal announcement. In fact, as we will see, present and past become relatively undifferentiated and can even share the same panel space in his work (see chap. 1). Yet here the diagonal sequence of canted panels has a clear psychological motivation.

The protagonist's movement in each of these panel frames establishes a clear vector diagonally downward toward the bottom-right page corner. In each one, the protagonist waves a piece of paper he has held since the panel where he changed his studies to refrigeration. Kinetic lines and dotted shadowing indicate his tight grasp on the paper. These formal elements emphasize the obsessive nature of his quest, which spills over diagonally into the large splash panel below—first in the "Union Made Amalgamated 102" insignia and, below that, the figure of the protagonist himself as he discovers the warehouse storing the pushcarts.

The insignia is visual evidence of his conclusion that "a secret union exists among these men." It appears out of time and space, thus as more of a mental image than a tactile object. This becomes particularly clear when it is compared to the "Kelso Dry Ice" or the "Ciro Wholesale Italian" tags appearing on the next page, both of which are depicted in the character's grasp within point-of-view panels. In fact, as we will see, Katchor frequently references unions in his work. Here as elsewhere their existence reflects the historical reality that such forms of sociality were important for both immigrant communities and the urban working class in New York. On this page, the Amalgamated 102 seems to promise the protagonist a form of fraternal bond that, we presume, he has not found in his mechanics studies. The insignia's position above his head—lifted out of the diegetic time and space of the comic—gives the impression that it is one more thought balloon, or a further intruding narration, in the diagonal series. It signifies the man's hope of a remedy for his urban alienation.[25]

In sum, "Italian Ices" is both a psychological character study and a quintessentially urban tale. The story relies almost certainly on Pavlovian associations between hot New York summers and the promise of a refreshingly cold treat, something with which many readers will easily identify. It is formally ambitious in a way that accentuates the psychology of its main character. There is at once something brave and pathetic about this obsessive protagonist, who bucks tradition and family expectations, who is willing to pound the city's streets day and night to make something of himself, only to retreat from his own dream in the end. Katchor's interest in the character conveys something about the vastness and complexity of the urban environment. His narrative suggests extended spatial and temporal dimensions through the presentation of decentralized business networks and mythologized origin tales dating far back in time. Yet mediating these two dimensions are the sights, sounds, and even tastes of life in the urban sensorium.

Comics Architecture

Modern comics are in many ways an urban medium.[26] The terms we use to talk about the comics page are urban and architectural—one may speak of the comics grid pattern and the comics gutter between panels. The way a comics page is structured can be described in architectural terms.[27] Katchor's work can be highly innovative in this sense. From the Julius Knipl strips of the 1980s and '90s through the pages he created for *Metropolis* magazine, Katchor conveys a preference for architecture not merely in the urban backgrounds of his comics but also in their themes and composition. This next example, published in Spiegelman and Mouly's *Raw* magazine (2, no. 2, [1990]) but composed for the magazine in 1989, shows the artist at his most creative, matching his interest in architecture as urban context and theme with an architectural approach to page design.

"The Corner Location" (1989) is a three-page work that actually consists of two distinguishable comics, two intersecting stories, that can be read top to bottom and traced from one page to the next. Both stories unfold in relation to a single building location on the corner of a city street. Each has a distinct title: on the verso is "The Collapsible Table Company," and on the recto is "The Drink of Life." This parallel structure appears in Katchor's other comics: "The Carbon Copy Building" (*HDA*, 10) and "Euro Trash / American Garbage" (*HDA*, 58; see chap. 2), for example, each of which consists of relatively autonomous stories that share the same page. "What Bruno Yule Heard" (*HDA*, 34) even consists of three such side-by-side strips. Here, however, Katchor's design is somewhat more ambitious. The conceit is that the two story lines also connect up in the final row of each page. They are merged in a wide panel that spans the magazine's fold at the bottom of each double page. Thus, in the final rows of each two-page spread, the characters from each story share the same space. They can see each other and, in principle at least, hear each other. The way in which the two stories are in communication with each other once again showcases Katchor's interest in using the comics form to contemplate the nature of the urban experience.

The verso tale, "The Collapsible Table Company," dramatizes the trials and tribulations of a door-to-door folding-table salesman. In the first two rows of the first page, readers see him giving his spiel, dealing with rejection, and talking to himself to cope (fig. I.3). After a hard day—at the bottom of the first page—he enters the corner business, which is named "The Drink of Life," and enjoys a beverage. The recto tale ("The Drink of Life," half of the comic) follows a new business owner as he acquires this beverage property, makes minor changes, and reaps the rewards of setting up at such an advantageous location. In the central panel of the bottom row, the previous owner looks left across the page fold, sees the table salesman of "The Collapsible Table Company" enjoying his drink, and tells the new owner encouragingly, "He's a regular . . . You see, there's a thirst that cannot be quenched by ordinary water."

The comic's architectural and urban aspects are primary. The bottom row functions well as the view from street level, and when taken in at a glance,[28] the upper rows of panels appear to rest on top of this street view as if they were the higher floors of a mixed-use building. Katchor complements the horizontal and vertical reading dimensions of the comic by introducing an anomaly that hints at a third dimension of depth. This anomaly is an embedded three-panel minicomic. Each of the three pages of "The Corner Location" has a central panel that hovers above the rest. As in the case of the insignia from "Italian Ices," these panels seem to exist outside of time and space, as mental representations, or what might be considered subjective shots in cinema. These three central

Fig. I.3. Ben Katchor, first page of the three-page comic "The Corner Location" (1989), *RAW* 2, no. 2 (1990): 180–82, published by Penguin Books. Reprinted with the generous permission of Ben Katchor.

LOCATION

The Drink of Life

The Collapsible Table Company *(continued)*

Fig. I.4. Ben Katchor, second page of "The Corner Location" (1989), *RAW* 2, no. 2 (1990): 180–82, published by Penguin Books. Reprinted with the generous permission of Ben Katchor.

The Drink of Life *(continued)*

panels share distinguishing features, or rather, a lack of certain features. They are bereft of detail, shading, and background. We see, on page 1, the salesman assembling the folding table in an otherwise empty white room. On page 2, the same panel frame exists in the same location on the page (fig. I.4). The salesman is no longer visible, and the table is set up, standing on four legs in the same empty white room. On page 3, the panel is still there, but the room is an empty, purely geometrical space. Neither the salesman nor the table can be seen. Through these three single panels, Katchor turns the regular beat of the three-panel strip into something much more complex.

In these two strips—three, actually, if one agrees that the minicomic stands on its own—Katchor pulls from his interests in the quintessentially urban themes of loneliness and connection, of work and leisure. Even the bare-bones minicomic is an expression of Katchor's preferred themes: the transitory nature of urban life, the feeling or the memory that lingers on after an object, or a person, has disappeared. The way he puts the verso and the recto stories in communication with their complement, by having them share the same page, conveys a multivocal quality or a "neighborhood feeling" that would not be present in an isolated single strip. These are smaller stories participating in a larger narrative about city life. This general idea also flows logically from the choice of subject. An urban corner is the node that puts each of two streets in communication with the other. Katchor's building and page design emphasizes two points of entry and exit in the ground-level business, thus one on each street. The final row on page 3 of the comic is bookended by two narrow panels: the verso shows the salesman entering The Drink of Life, and the recto shows the owner leaving the same business by a different door. The architecture of the building and the architecture of the comics page are in tune.

"The Corner Location" serves in practical terms as a crossroads or a meeting point for different people. Symbolically, it is a showcase of different urban stories, diverse ways of living. This is the idea of the city itself as the site of difference. In the material city, understood as a lived space, one turns a corner and never knows what one might find. The urban phenomenon can be defined, in fact, as being synonymous with difference and diversity. Katchor turns this hallmark unpredictability, diversity, and connectivity of city life into a masterful comic by emphasizing the fold on the page and incorporating it into the comic's diegesis.

On the comic's first page, the fold of the page marks the corner of the titular building, a decision by Katchor that takes the notion of comics architecture to an extreme; on the second page, the fold marks the corner of the countertop in the building's first-floor interior. This match along the page fold also plays into the central page image where the salesman sets up his table. On both pages where the table appears, its own fold is also aligned with the page crease. The actions of the salesman thus mirror the actions necessary for readers to engage with the materiality of the print issue of *Raw*. As readers fold and unfold the comics magazine in the course of reading, they perform physical actions in sync with the table salesman in Katchor's story. This resonance between the diegetic world of the comic and the world of its readers surely makes "The Corner Location" one of the most innovative in the artist's repertoire, and arguably, too, one of the most innovative in American comics.[29]

At the same time, "The Corner Location" fits squarely within Katchor's preferred set of urban themes. The takeaway message, as voiced by the new owner of The Drink of Life in the final panel, is that "in this business all you need is a good location." The comics artist is attentive throughout his works to the way in which city locations are in fact commodities. Good locations make for successful businesses, while poor locations make for unsuccessful ones. A complementary, if inverse, message can be found in the strip "The Vacant Store Front" (*BSD*, 23), wherein "a rare combination of poor location and high rent" is the cause for "the oldest continually vacant storefront in America! . . . It's the Grand Canyon of commercial undesirability." The urban environment is an uneven geography when it comes to commerce. While small businesses seek an advantageous location, the value of a location can more easily be harnessed by speculators and capitalists, as is dramatized in strips such as "A Look at the Poleax Building" (*HDA*, 45).

All things considered, Katchor is equally attuned to the temporal dimension of cities. This temporal aspect is subdued in "The Corner Location," as Katchor spends more time with the connective spatial dimension of architecture and the beginning moments of a new business acquisition. Yet elsewhere he seems to think through the uncertain future of a business like The Drink of Life soda fountain dispensary. In one strip collected in *Cheap Novelties*, Julius Knipl's search for a fountain drink he used to enjoy is fruitless. The narrator channels the character's disappointment into historical reflections and asks a rhetorical question: "As one soda fountain drink was born / Another would fade into oblivion"; "Can a certain combination of carbonated water / syrup / and that unlikely third ingredient / command the palate of a fickle public"? (*CN*, 51). As with this example involving literal taste, the comics artist's sustained forays into the world of real estate also serve to dramatize the ephemeral nature of trends concerning figurative taste. In a page for *Metropolis* magazine titled "Open House Season" (*HDA*, 7), a pair of city dwellers visit twelve or more open houses each Sunday with no intention of buying a property, merely to enjoy the visual consumption of the latest in living arrangements. In another, Katchor takes the idea of "The Deep Tub" (*HDA*, 68) to an illogical extreme, again poking fun at the fickle consumer's desires.

Katchor's comics prompt readers to confront an unflattering but thoroughly realistic idea of the general public—people who have a short memory and are ruled by manufactured whims. "The Corner Location" is no exception to this. Its premise is that a great location makes up even for a lousy or unnecessary product. On the first recto page of the comic, the business's previous owner points out that there is a functioning public water fountain right across the street, and states defiantly that "the Drink of Life" is "a lousy product . . . but they still come to buy it." The salesman from the neighboring strip "The Collapsible Table Company" is himself "duped" into buying "the Drink of Life"—by architectural proximity if not also by a consumeristic thirst for a novel product. Over the course of three pages, we see him progressively conditioned to buy the beverage after a hard day's work, so much so that this repetition reduces him to little more than his own mechanical response. Still, he also gets something out of the experience. Thus Katchor conveys the dual role of architecture and, by extension, of the city. It controls us, habituates and conditions us, but the urban environment also provides opportunities for release, conversation, connection, and perhaps—through spontaneity and sensory pleasures—even a momentary joy.

CHAPTER 1

Sight

E ven the quickest of surveys will reveal that Ben Katchor's most enduring and even endearing character is Julius Knipl. Strictly speaking, Knipl may not be a New Yorker, but he certainly reads that way. (Katchor has insisted that any relevance to New York is purely coincidental in the strip.) Critics have described Knipl as "a quintessentially urban figure," an "unlikely urban archaeologist," and "a Whitmanian wanderer," who plods the streets of a large, fictionalized city with "his Box Brownie camera strapped to his back like a pilgrim's knapsack."[1] In a word, he is a flâneur. Detached from the hustle and bustle of the city, Knipl floats along deserted alleys, passing just as unaffected through the teeming urban crowd, solitary, always contemplative. His name comes from "the Yiddish word for little treasure to put away for a rainy day, little nest-egg that the palm of your mind can hold."[2] His photographic eye captures the small details of this urban life that others are content to ignore.

Julius Knipl's profession seems at once grandiose and marginal. Just what is a real estate photographer? His creator has explained:

> I didn't really know too much about what it meant except that people take utilitarian photographs of buildings for brokers to use for owners to show. I thought it was a strange business because it combines two professions that have all sorts of powerful connotations: real estate and photography and yet it's a kind of pathetic profession, a man that goes around taking utilitarian photographs.[3]

Of course, readers seldom see Knipl take a photograph. From the beginning, his attempts are frustrated. In the first strip collected in *Cheap Novelties*, he gets quite close to photographing the Goulash Building but then has to wait for the shadows to "be just right" (*CN*, 5). We never see him snap. Soon afterward, his shot of a different building's facade is delayed by the presence of a crowd (7). Then an injured mover gets in the way of Knipl's shot; the man has fallen under the weight of a piano he has been tasked with carrying on his own, a reference to a classic comics gag (10). At still another location, we are rewarded with an onomatopoeic "clic" right at the moment that a newspaper obscures Knipl's lens, lifted up by an unexpected wind (*CN*, 12). No matter. He is less interested in his photographs than he is in the small corners of the city he happens upon during his frequent strolls.

Indeed, Knipl may be "less a character than a motive or perhaps an alibi for Katchor to reflect on the city."[4] And we are all too eager to reflect with him. Through the frames of many a comics panel, we stare with him at the forgotten marginalia the city has to offer. Parading through the image and text zones of the strips are discarded objects, overheard conversations, and a slew of "crackpot inventors with schemes for achieving success."[5] The prevailing theme is nostalgia. It is an introspective comic, imbued with a philosophical tone. Still, Katchor's urban reflections reach toward economic and political concerns as well. He once explained the Julius Knipl strips by saying, "I tried to invest the workings of the market economy as I'd observed or imagined them with a poetic logic."[6]

Despite the strip's heady subject matter, or perhaps because of it, Julius Knipl achieved syndication in various independent weekly papers across the United States. Among its first homes in the late 1980s were the *New York Press* and *The Forward*. Katchor's father had a subscription to "the *Freiheit*, the Yiddish-language Communist daily paper," which was founded in 1922, but *The Forward* was surely also a point of reference for the wider circles in which he would have moved.[7] The *Forverts*, as the Yiddish-language

Jewish Daily Forward was known, was established in 1897 and by 1910 "had become the most widely read Yiddish newspaper in the world and the most important Socialist daily in the country."[8] The time period in which the Knipl strips take place may very well be the 1950s to 1970s of Ben Katchor's youth, but what one critic has called their "piquant nostalgia for vanished labor and obsolete microeconomies" recalls labor struggles from a number of periods in American history.[9]

The existing scholarship on Julius Knipl has tended to focus on Katchor's portrayal of a dilapidated urban world, full of forgotten, unused, and largely unseen items. Undoubtedly, "nostalgia, desire and even memory" are among his core themes.[10] But repeating this mantra risks underplaying the complexity and range of his comics storytelling. Nostalgia is not indulged merely for its own sake. Instead the strips push readers to recognize the ethical and economic dimensions of urban life. As this chapter explores, these dimensions are particularly evident when his comics emphasize the power of what is seen or not seen.

In two examples taken from the Julius Knipl strips, we gain a sense of how Katchor wants us to see differently. Analysis centers both on the role of drawn architecture in his panels and also on the interesting way in which his comics composition privileges visual memory. Next, a strip published in *Hand-Drying in America* provides an example of how what is seen can acquire explicitly sociopolitical dimensions. "Passing Through" is a story that pits labor versus management, pushing us to look differently at working relationships—to see them for what they are, which is systematically exploitative. Finally, in "The Lambswoll Hotel," a selection from the *Hotel & Farm* series, he uses the visual sense as a prompt for critiquing the way in which even our individual lives have become commodities. The strip's critical humor sits uncomfortably with the reality that media, spectacle, and patterns of consumption have evolved in tandem and now threaten to supplant human relations.[11]

The Persistence of Memory

Katchor's work is certainly concerned with the aporias of time, with disappearances, with the notion of a city that no longer exists. One of the artist's main insights regards the strength of our felt connections to place. Such feelings linger long after a given stimulus has disappeared. To read his comics work as a paean for the times of old, however, is a betrayal. They hardly amount to a sepia-tone wash of historical complexity. The artist does not want us to return to a kind of premodern urbanity that was somehow more authentic. In fact, the strips collected in *The Cardboard Valise* can be thought of in just this way—as a drawn critique of the static, frozen, or somehow "authentic" views of local history and culture that are marketed to travelers.[12] Instead, the Julius Knipl strips use the past to critique social relationships that reveal themselves in the present. What we see on the page is the visual echo of a bygone city, one that nonetheless offers up lessons about our present-day indifference, ignorance, and urban alienation.

What sets Knipl apart from other urbanites is his ability to see differently and to connect sight with thinking. This is not always easy to do in the modern metropolis. Already in 1903, in the essay "The Metropolis and Mental Life," Georg Simmel noted that the urban environment was characterized by an overstimulation of the senses—much of it having to do with excessive visual spectacle. To cope with this psychological overload, Simmel explained, modern city dwellers must cultivate a state of indifference, a blasé attitude, regarding what they see and hear. As Katchor's strips bear out, it is but a short step from indifference to ignorance. Our sense of sight can become dulled by overexposure to urban spectacle. The punch line from one of Katchor's strips in *Cheap Novelties* has a discount store cashier first notice the color of the floor of the place where he stands daily only after he has been working there five years (*CN*, 76). We are generally conditioned to tune out the world around us.

A strip focusing on the Kozma Theater uses visual signage to probe beyond the surface of what we see in the city (*CN*, 52; see fig. 1.1). Aesthetically, this strip shares many qualities with the other Julius Knipl comics collected in *Cheap Novelties*. It features a black-and-white composition with gray shading and a breakdown that spans eight to ten individual panels arranged in two vertical rows, and it begins with a curious object floating above the first, upper-left panel. These objects are consistently imprinted with the name Julius Knipl and his professional title of Real Estate Photographer. Presumably, they are to be given away as advertising for his services. Some are true novelties: a snow globe, a desk gong, a rabbit's foot, a Chinese finger trap, a maze containing balls of mercury, a small harmonica. Some are seemingly more useful: an umbrella, a can opener, a clothespin, an eraser, a belt buckle, a doorstop. Others are perhaps less useful: Knipl-branded men's underwear. These are visual reminders, and by suggestion also tactile affirmations, of a midcentury small-business sales economy. Their significance is arguably more concentrated for readers who have Katchor's entire collection of strips at their fingertips. The sheer number of these objects (a quick count yields eighty-six such items) and their repetition throughout the volume suggest an anxiety about the pressures of working in sales. They convey a weariness that comes from having to pound the pavement to personally solicit paying customers.[13]

The object at upper left in the Kozma Theater strip is a lollipop; Knipl's business information is stamped on the treat's cellophane wrapper. As with the union insignia in the "Italian Ices" story, the lollipop hovers above the panel content, as if it somehow existed outside of time and space. Its branding imprint leaves no doubt that it connects with the diegetic world of the comic's story line. Yet its ontological status is imprecise. Is this an actual object that Knipl has bought in bulk to support the expansion of his business? Or is it an idea that got left on the drafting table, so to speak, and therefore more of a dream than a reality? Along with its companion objects, those distributed across the other strips in the volume, the

Fig. 1.1 Ben Katchor, "The Kozma Theater," in *Cheap Novelties* (Drawn & Quarterly, 2016), 52. Reprinted with the generous permission of Ben Katchor.

lollipop expresses Katchor's idea of infusing the market economy with what he called "a poetic logic." Its visual disjunction relative to the comic's empaneled content suggests the diffuse connections between materiality and consciousness, between the object world that can be seen (and touched) and the subjective world of less-tangible thoughts, memories, dreams, and ambitions.

The strip begins with Julius Knipl in mid-stroll, staring at a series of storefronts bearing similar names: the Kozma Luncheonette, the Kozma Bakery, Kozma Menswear, Kozma Pizza, the Kozma Arms, and Kozma Drugs (*CN*, 52). Katchor's use of light and shadow emphasizes that our urban flâneur makes sure to stay out of the sun's rays. Perhaps the comfort of the shady side of the street is more conducive to thinking. This consistent use of light and shadow in the first six panels paves the way for the climactic seventh panel. Along the way, Knipl's word balloons signal that he is indulging in a memory: "Everyone wanted to cash in on that name. / I remember the Kozma." But most of the text zones here are taken up by the narrator's ruminations. This third-person narrator echoes Knipl's state of mind and even anticipates his memory. Although this narration has access to Knipl's inner thoughts, it has a distinct voice. It is comparatively verbose and more contemplative, offering up a concise lesson steeped in urban history: "A small business would thrive just because of its proximity to the place. / It was a landmark / known by name throughout the city." This commentary adds a degree of emotional texture and perhaps a bit of offbeat humor: "Now, it [Kozma] is a painfully strange appellation / befitting a river in Eastern Europe or a patented coffee substitute." By contrast, the protagonist's observation sticks to the basic facts: "A big theater on that corner / They knocked it down six years ago."

The penultimate panel—here, the seventh of eight—carries the punctuating beat of the comic. The artist's stylistic and formal choices reveal the nuanced relationship that his comics nurture between the past and the present. The composition of the panel blends foreground with background, and thus present with past, with no strong distinction. Katchor gives no formal indication that we are seeing the past. That is, there is no thought balloon containing an image, no internal panel or inset, no line internal to the frame, whatsoever. Instead readers see Knipl's back in the foreground as he stares at an image of the Kozma theater. We know this is Knipl in the present, not in the past, because of his word balloon, whose stream of consciousness self-talk extends across all the panels in the comic's second row. We also know that this image of the Kozma theater is in the past, not the present, because of the use of light in the sixth, seventh, and eighth frames. The seventh panel marks a shift from day to night, with the interior light of the theater's lobby spilling out onto the darkness of the front sidewalk. As Knipl remembers the Kozma as it used to be, he sees it—and we see it—as it once was, not in his mind's eye so much as in reality, how it actually looked. The facade's detail and the lighting are instrumental to this effect: urban memory is rendered on the page with all the authority of an actual past image.

This comic offers a prime example of the "slow, contemplative walkabouts" for which Katchor is known.[14] The story's gradual development through its penultimate panel allows us to actually see the continuing influence of the city's past on its present. An urban lesson is offered up to readers through a sort of symbiotic storytelling, which is achieved through the coparticipation of Knipl and the third-person narrator. What urbanites might otherwise take to be isolated businesses are in fact part of an organic ecosystem. Katchor juxtaposes surface (the storefront signage) and depth (the light emanating from the theater) in the comic's visual architectural language to reinforce this idea: one must see things in deep urban time.

This temporal effect—the artist's decision to blend present and past within the panel frame without a strong distinction—appears in many of his comics. Its use goes far beyond the Knipl strips, appearing also in his other collections. In a strip from *The Cardboard Valise*, for instance, Katchor uses the same effect (*CV*, 14). In its first panel, a couple begins to narrate a story. Their heads are pushed low in the foreground (present), while the story they are telling is illustrated behind them in the background (past), with no formal distinction. An additional device is used. The stems of the word balloons carrying their narration emanate from the diegetic space outside the panel frame, maintaining the illusion that they are still in the foreground, this time in the adjacent off-panel space.[15]

One of the strips collected in *The Beauty Supply District* provides another most interesting example of Katchor's preference for direct images of the past. This eight-panel strip titled "Jubilation Alley" (*BSD*, 51; see fig. 1.2) combines the unmarked blending of present foreground and past background, as explored in the example of the Kozma Theater strip, with off-panel word balloon emanations, as just noted in the example from *The Cardboard Valise*.

The theme of "Jubilation Alley" is urban joy. Katchor underscores this idea in the very title of the comic but also threads it through the story line. The strip's title is also the title of the novel embedded in the story, *Jubilation Alley*, written by the fictitious author Constantine Hoople. While riding the subway, Knipl's hallmark eye for detail prompts a discussion about the book with the young man sitting next to him. Surely he is being nosy by reading over the man's shoulder, given that—as made clear by both the images and the dialogue of the strip—the book's identity is obscured by a Christmas wrapping paper cover. Whereas one can only speculate what the embedded novel itself is about, urban joy figures into much of the strip's action. First, there is the joy of a spontaneous encounter leading to a gratifying conversation while on the train. This is underscored by the narrator's only text box, which notes that Knipl has happened to sit down next to the young man "by chance." The liveliness of their conversation is further emphasized through visual contrast with the immobile passengers standing and sitting on either side of them. Beyond the shared joy of a conversation with a stranger, there is also the specific joy of reading, if not also the general joy of having a private moment despite being surrounded by the urban multitude.

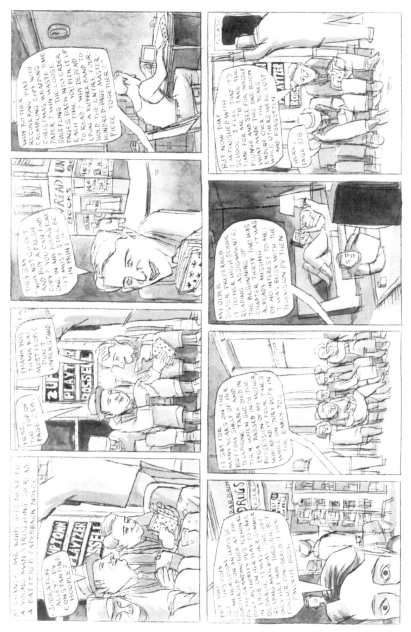

Fig 1.2. Ben Katchor, "Jubilation Alley," in *The Beauty Supply District* (Pantheon Books, 2000), 51. Reprinted with the generous permission of Ben Katchor.

The deeper joy of the strip, however, lies in the story that the young reader tells Knipl. No doubt speaking to Knipl's heart, the youth's story reveals that the *Jubilation Alley* novel is essentially a knipl. His grandmother purchased it at the Port Authority bus terminal in 1958 on a trip. Though she only got halfway through it, she "considered it her favorite book." It then passed to the young man's mother, "who read it four times while on jury duty in the early 70s." Later, his sister preferred to read it during her high school days instead of doing her homework—even though chapter 32 was missing. The variation and irregularity of these reading practices only endear the book to the young man more. The book's use value seems only to increase over time, despite its progressive physical deterioration. The latter is emphasized by the semiregular beats of Julius Knipl's interjections: "Here, the top of page 218" (panel 2), he says, while handing the youth a fallen page, and again later, "Here, page 378" (panel 8). The decrepit book with its pages falling out is a reminder that joy is both real and ephemeral.

The images in panels 3 through 7 are all related to the young man's narration. The *Jubilation Alley* novel is an obscure but prized family possession. As we learn more of the book's history, a close-up view of wide eyes and the storyteller's forehead conveys his excitement over this "heirloom purchased on an impulse." The scene in the background of panel 5 is a past image of his grandmother picking the book off a discount rack in the station. This is unlikely to be a memory that the young man would have, and it makes more sense to interpret the scene, in the context of Katchor's oeuvre, as a direct image of the past. The artist's urban spaces seem to have their own memories; they act as anchors for meaningful acts executed in the past, and—like his third-person narrators—they share an unexplained connection with the central urbanites of his comics stories. Earlier, in panel 3, the young man's torso occupied the foreground while the background showed a more distant view of his grandmother in the bookstore. Between panels 3 and 5, the visual narration of the comic thus effects a zoom, enlarging the direct past image of the bookstore.[16] This enlargement of the past also involves an enlargement of the present (panel 5 is drawn closer to the young man's face), such that readers understand that a certain tension exists between the two time periods. The strip's deeper implication is consistent with lessons offered in the artist's other strips: the past never entirely disappears; it is only that we have neglected its memory. The past is all around us in the present, if only we know how to see it.

Seeing What Is Hidden

Katchor's interest in what we see or do not see is not restricted to matters of the past. He has spoken in interviews of wanting to get away from the old-new dichotomy of urban depictions. By moving beyond the limitations of nostalgia, he is able to examine contemporary social relations more carefully. In his words, what he is most interested in is

> reinventing the possibilities of the city, rather than just nostalgia for an old city. Oh, it's all gone! Or how wonderful everything new is—that's the other approach. I wanted to reinvent the possibility of a city. They tend to be capitalist cities, though I think I've written stories about utopian communes.[17]

One full-page, color strip from *Hand-Drying in America* in particular showcases his commitment to creating a more socially and economically just world. While the plot focuses on labor inequities in the context of a specific restaurant, the third-person narration encourages readers to view the story in allegorical perspective.

"Passing Through" (*HDA*, 152), which was originally published in the *Metropolis* architecture magazine, is as urban in subject matter as any of the artist's other strips. The title itself has both an urban and an architectural meaning. On the urban side, it hints at the same themes of spontaneity and felicitous if ephemeral encounters just discussed in the case of "Jubilation Alley"—hallmarks of the urban experience. By chance, the main character stumbles upon a "modest Etruscan restaurant," where he orders pork liver with bay leaves. It seems he is just passing through and enjoying a nice day on the town. His name, Francis Gallstone, calls to mind a bodily organ known to serve as the stage for its own kind of painful passing. The pain in the comic is primarily social, however. While passing through the restaurant, Gallstone's presence exacerbates the schism between the restaurant's kitchen staff and its on-site manager. By the strip's final row of panels, an uprising of sorts has occurred. In the final panel, the staff carries the manager out of the restaurant. His arms are spread wide, suggesting a pose of tragic sacrifice. Gallstone has finally passed through.

On the architectural side of things, the strip's title refers to the pass-through, a small window separating the kitchen from the dining room of a restaurant. This little window is seen in the comic's first panel and exercises a disproportionate influence on both the plot and the composition of the strip (fig. 1.3).

The strip's story hinges on the fact that the pass-through is left open, allowing Gallstone to see into the kitchen. What follows is a moment of disalienation that prompts a surge of social consciousness. Under normal circumstances, diners in a restaurant are separated from the area where their food is being prepared. Consequently, as Katchor sees it, they are ignorant of the labor conditions that have produced the value of their meals. A single moment is all it takes to effect a lasting change: "Francis Gallstone catches a glimpse into the kitchen. / What he sees alters his understanding of the labor involved in preparing his meal." What the narration describes as "the simple architectural expedient of a 'pass-through'—an opening between two rooms fitted with a shelf and sliding window" becomes a catalyst to revolution. Both Gallstone and the narrator alike are driven to Marxist rhetoric: the former says, "Brothers, you have nothing to lose but your chains!" and "Together we'll assume communal ownership of the restaurant!"; the latter, "All social relations are radically altered

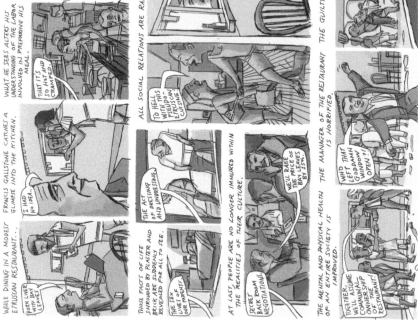

Fig. 1.3. Ben Katchor, "Passing Through," in *Hand-Drying in America* (Pantheon Books, 2013), 152. Reprinted with the generous permission of Ben Katchor.

for the better," and "The mental and physical health of an entire society is improved."

Compositionally speaking, the pass-through casts a long shadow. It appears in seven different panels of the strip. The window is present in the first panel, though none of the kitchen figures are visible. In the second panel, the pass-through frames a kitchen employee in a tight midshot. This architectural comics framing signifies the employee's lack of social power in the restaurant, his reduction by the larger economic forces of profit seeking. Still, Katchor carries the idea further by adapting the pass-through to a kind of visual metaphor in panels 5, 6, and 7. These panels are contemplative digressions from the strip's main action. In panel 5, the outline of the pass-through can still be seen, but it opens up into a domestic interior as the words voiced in tandem by the narrator and Gallstone meditate on what walls keep private: "the sex lives of our parents / the act of dressing and undressing / secret back room negotiations." What happens, the strip asks, if "those facts of life shrouded by plaster and brick are suddenly revealed for all to see"?

Katchor's use of color cues readers to understand that a shift is taking place in the narration. While the wall in the restaurant where the pass-through is located is blue in panel 1, this group of three panels in the middle row instead uses bluish tones for the imagined interior scenes they contain. This inversion is purposeful and can be tied to the comic's theme of inverted social hierarchies. Color is also used to contrast the restaurant's dining room with the kitchen's interior, and thus the sphere of consumption with the sphere of production. Panels 3 and 8 employ reddish hues to convey the physical heat of the restaurant kitchen and also the rising temperature of a fomented revolution.

One of the most interesting panels is the fourth, which offers a reverse view back into the dining room from the kitchen. In this panel, readers are placed in the position of the restaurant's working underclass. The pass-through appears here as a framing device internal to the comics panel. By contrast with how much of the kitchen employee readers can see in panel 2, here Gallstone is allowed a more expansive framing. The bright, clear lighting of the dining room now connotes privilege and opulence. As readers meet Gallstone's gaze, which has been painted as sympathetic by the overarching third-person narration, they understand that a new social contract is being forged. A reversal in formal perspective at the level of composition anticipates of the reversal of social inequality at the level of the comic's action. More than that, Katchor establishes a sympathy between architectural form and comics form. The strip grants the reader access to spaces that are not normally seen in comics but are internal to the frame.[18]

Although "Passing Through" is one of the most formally interesting of his comics, it is hardly the only one to deal with themes of social alienation or exploitative labor. On the inside cover of *Hand-Drying in America*, Katchor takes on exploitation in the global printing industry, noting that "here skilled labor is cheap and plentiful," and having "no union troubles" keeps costs of printing cheap and the profit margin high. In a strip from *The Cardboard Valise*, an industrial plant guide cuts a guest tour short, saying, "We hope to keep this information from the general consumer public. They are better off not knowing the details of our manufacturing processes, thank you" (*CV*, 33). "Passing Through" seems lighter than those two examples. We find a touch of humor in its last panel, where Katchor suggests how easily the apparatus of power can fall in the context of an individual restaurant. "The guilty waiter [who] relaxes outside with a cigarette" has presumably left the pass-through window open on purpose, allowing Gallstone visual access to the kitchen and precipitating the entire chain of events. Radical consciousness arises as the result of the spontaneous—mechanical and all too quotidian—use of an architectural feature. This finale reasserts one of Katchor's central themes: we are all "victims" of design. As urbanites we are beholden to it and conditioned by what it allows us to see or not see.

The Lives of Others

The comic just discussed is hardly the only example of how Katchor's comics cultivate a critical consciousness regarding economic forces. His urban depictions bring the more risible, absurd, and exploitative qualities of the market economy to life. One thinks, perhaps, of trade in *The Jew of New York*, of signage and advertising in *The Beauty Supply District*, or of manufacturing in *Hand-Drying in America*, but in truth these themes are threaded throughout all his works. Beyond these classic economic associations, he is also attuned to more recent developments in the context of a postwar consumer culture.

Katchor's comics reflect insights from the interdisciplinary terrain of urban studies.[19] The first is that the city itself became a commodity in the nineteenth century. In a strip from *Hand-Drying in America*, for example, the powerful Poleax Corporation monetizes its central location to charge passersby on the street who happen to look up at the building ("A Look at the Poleax Building," *HDA*, 45). The result is a humorous take on the way in which the monopoly rent of unique locations has been harnessed by speculators and developers in large cities.

The second insight of note is that in the twentieth century, everyday life has been colonized as a strategy of capital accumulation. Katchor plays with this idea, mixing it with the slapdash get-rich-quick schemes of small-time inventors (see also figs. 4.1, 4.2). In "The After-Rain Business" (*BSD*, 41), one such crackpot speculates on how "there is a potential source of income hidden within each manifestation of nature." While the response to rain has been "a vast industry of umbrellas, water-proof coats and rubber shoes," no one has yet tapped the post-rain market. In the last panel comes a most impractical idea: "The puddles on the main thorough-fares of this city have yet to be mapped and charted." Later, "De Vowel's Water-proof Puddle Map" appears as a found-object illustration in the back of the collection. An equally absurd strip called "The Crumb Trap" (*HDA*, 54) proposes that there is profit to be made by collecting the crumbs from the city's toaster ovens. Sorting them by size and quality—into small, medium, and large crumbs, burned crumbs, and sharp crumbs—one has acquired a raw material that can then be sold for use in disparate products and services (e.g., breading for chicken nuggets, a compound for janitorial work, fuel for heating public night schools, etc.).

The idea that our everyday life provides raw materials that can be leveraged for profit is also a central part of business in our image-obsessed contemporary society (think Facebook, Instagram, and the like). Katchor has designed his strip "The Lambswoll Hotel" as a commentary on this newer form of the market economy. Originally the strip was part of the *Hotel & Farm* series, in which the creator alternated between urban and rural settings, between hotels and farms, perhaps influenced by the fact that his father at one point ran a "small hotel and chicken farm."[20] While selected other comics from the *Hotel & Farm* series appeared in an issue of *Art Journal* (2002), this particular strip was republished in the comics issue of *McSweeney's Quarterly Concern*, no. 13 (2004), guest edited by Chris Ware.

The novel idea dramatized in "The Lambswoll Hotel" (*H&F*, 173) is that a certain kind of channel is being offered to hotel guests as a "new form of in-room entertainment." From the comfort of the hotel bed, it is now possible to watch recordings of the previous occupants of the same room in which a guest is staying the night: "For an additional $12., discreetly billed to your account, we offer histories of the room's three previous occupants. Learn who left that cigarette burn in your blanket; discover whose dresses hung on your hangers; who bathed in your tub . . ." (fig. 1.4). This humorous exercise in voyeurism caters to the fact that "our guests are naturally curious," as the hotel waiter says, and this curiosity is rewarded with a slew of banal details. Of the previous guest named "Harrison Jove" ("Estimated Age: 47, Pharmaceutical Salesman, Morsil, IL"), we learn what he ordered from room service ("Veal Scallopini, Vanilla Ice Cream, Texas Omelet"), and what he consumed from the room's refrigerator ("Three Ginger Ales, Spanish

Peanuts . . ."). One passive guest watches another passive guest, often with misanthropic disgust ("The fat slob. I can just see him lounging on this bed. Ugh!").

The comic functions as a mise en abyme. Harrison Jove is confined to the frame of the room's television, the current guest who watches him on the screen is confined to his hotel room, and we view his passive complacency through the confines of the strip's panels. Television screens appear in four of the eight panels, and audio can be heard in another three, multiplying the effect of the theme of viewership. In the last panel of the first row, the frame of the television approximates the panel frame, collapsing the world of storytelling and the world of the reader. At both levels, visual spectacle induces passive spectatorship, and passive spectatorship reproduces itself. Media consumption has colonized our daily lives while offering us merely an unremarkable vision of the quotidian. The second row's last panel is the only one to show an exterior wall and a window. The blinds are drawn up, and the rectangular view to the outside is blank, offering no distraction from our own descent into self-involved objectification.

Throughout the *Hotel & Farm* strips, Katchor's hotel names are suggestive: "Hotel Gastrula," for example, or "The Rankor Hotel" (see also the strip "Hotel Names" included in *Art Journal*). Here, the compound name used in "The Lambswoll Hotel" calls to mind an animal known for its passivity. Like lambs to the slaughter, the hotel's guests are sacrificed to media spectacle as both observers and those observed. Playing on the cozy associations of lambswool, here we have instead lamb-swoll. Should readers be alert for swollen lamb? If there is indeed a swelling involved, it would be that of the hotel guests' rotting critical faculties, which are largely unused and irrelevant. If "Passing Through" illustrates the potential of seeing differently, "The Lambswoll Hotel" uses what one critic has called "melancholy guests in decaying hotels" to signal its death.[21]

Fig. 1.4. Ben Katchor, "The Lambswoll Hotel," in "Hotel & Farm," selections collected in *McSweeney's Quarterly Concern*, no. 13 (2004): 173, published by Penguin Books. Reprinted with the generous permission of Ben Katchor.

CHAPTER 2

Hearing

Ben Katchor's interest in our sense of hearing is hardly casual. He understands that sound has an uncanny ability to move us. As we have learned from popular neuroscience, sound penetrates into the reptilian core of our brain, and into the central cortex that controls our bodily movements.[1] It is intimately wrapped up in our emotional life, cultural taste, and social development. In the form of music, for example, drawing on a long human history that ties sound to sociality, it can prompt visceral enjoyment. Accordingly, Katchor's comics frequently turn to sounds for their touches of humor, conceptual absurdities, and significance.

Myriad wanted and unwanted sounds saturate our modern urban environment. Noise in Katchor's comics comes in the form of both alerts and common annoyances. The strip titled "Twelve-Noon Siren" (*JK*, 57) has Julius Knipl imagining "that he can hear the plaintive cry of a twelve-noon siren" emanating from a shoehorn-manufacturing plant. The comic's visual narration cuts across various urban scenes, depicting those people within earshot, and it ends with Knipl's own hunger pangs—a Pavlovian response to the siren's "merciless blare" ("Wroooooooo"). In a strip from *The Cardboard Valise*, the character named Elijah Salamis declares that he has done what other city dwellers could only dream of doing. As a group of his devotees gather outside, ringing his doorbell ("Bbrrinnnnggg" / "Eennnghk"), Salamis reclines on his living-room chaise and declares, "I have untrained myself to associate that sound with the arrival of a visitor. The signal alarms of modern life—the ringing phone, the doorbell, the car horn—mean nothing to me" (*CV*, 44). Here is proof on the page that a seasoned city dweller can cultivate a blasé attitude in the midst of a chaotic urban soundscape.

The idea of sound as noise and annoyance is carried to an extreme in "The Faulty Switch" (*HDA*, 4), one of the first full-page strips Katchor made for *Metropolis* magazine. Here the artist dramatizes what happens when "another beautifully designed new building [is] ruined by the sound of the common wall light switch." He devotes no fewer than sixteen of the comic's twenty-three panels to various negative reactions to the switch's sound. When turned on, it is "crude" and "recalls to mind a dirty men's room." When it is turned off, it has a "deep melancholy ring." The narrator asks, "Is it an imitation of one-half the set of sound we make to express disappointment: the orphaned dental consonant of no Indo-European language? [readers see the words 'Tsk, tsk' in a woman's word balloon] / "Or, is it the amplified sound of a synapse firing in the brain of a cockroach?" The fact is that all the human suffering chronicled by Katchor's comic in its last three rows has been caused not by the building's architect but instead by a contractor who decides to buy cheap seventy-nine-cent switches. Readers of the magazine who are practicing architects are likely to feel they are off the hook.

Across his many decades of producing comics, Katchor has turned to music as a way of engaging in social commentary and dramatizing his more characteristically absurd themes. A strip collected in *The Cardboard Valise* has the character Elijah Salamis attend a midtown concert hall in the fictitious Fluxion City. There he offers a biting ethnomusicological critique of a local market for "the folk music of Pelagia" to anyone who will listen. In the end, however, for all his bluster, he is reduced to the status of a mere autograph-seeking fan (*CV*, 65). In "The Radiator Musician" (*JK*, 68), Katchor lampoons the musical avant-garde by chronicling an unusual series of solo winter concerts (e.g., "Fetor Maracas in an evening of steam lullabies. Apartment 3-G, 235 Vaytig Avenue at Eight"). In "The Beauty Supply District" (*BSD*, 85–108), an acclaimed avant-garde composer has built a convoluted mechanical instrument that passes a leather tongue delicately across the surface of cream. This tongue repeatedly displaces a portion onto a taut intestinal membrane. The sound it produces is much like a cat's tongue lapping up milk.[2] In addition, both the urban and the natural worlds offer their own music of a sort: a company markets the sound of the ocean to those who call its service (*CV*, 80), and an urbanite getting some rest is soothed by the sound of the "number seven uptown local" train as he drifts off to sleep in a rural asylum ("The Drowned Men's Association," *JK*, 1).

Sound can also prompt more profound sentiments—from the unexpected horror of a banal event to a tragic reflection on the significance of one's life. In one of the *Hotel & Farm* strips, a visitor to the U-Pick-Em! Cherry Farm is deeply affected by what he hears: "For the first time in his life, he's struck by the horrific sound of a fruit being torn from its stem" (*H&F*, 174). What promised to be a relaxing trip to the countryside for a quaint activity ends up leaving an invisible scar on the man's psyche: "The hollow knock of the fruit cadaver as it hits the bottom of the collecting pail turns his stomach." In the last panel, he loses his taste for fruit altogether. In a strip from *Cheap Novelties*, Julius Knipl observes a man who steps out from his apartment building "to stand in the street and have a good cough" (*CN*, 77). The narrator speaks on Knipl's behalf as he imagines a string of scenes whose connective tissue remains underdetermined. Playing like a filmstrip, the narration produces the idea that the sound of the man's cough carries with it events and images from his life. "In this deep resonant boom, Mr. Knipl can discern / the sound of a stickball bat connecting with a rubber ball / the sound of beer kegs rolling in the street / a time-clock stamping 5:08 p.m. / someone rifling through the pages of a men's magazine / the opening of a can of corned beef hash." In the last panel, the narration elucidates Knipl's thought balloon as he imagines "the sound of the police taking an apartment door off by its hinges." All these events are played on the screen of Julius Knipl's mind, much as the movie of a life lived in mediocrity and now reaching its final moments. The final image of the police breaking into the man's apartment hints that he will die alone and—perhaps the cherry on this tragic cake of a life lived in despair—remain undiscovered for a time.

Katchor's love for sound has also propelled him into the realm of musical theater, live performances based on his comics. Along with longtime collaborator Mark Mulcahy, Katchor has created musical theater inspired by his comics work and even by specific strips. These include *Up from the Stacks*, *A Checkroom Romance*, *The Rosenbach Company*, *The Slugbearers of Kayrol Island*, *Memorial City*, and *The Imaginary War Crimes Tribunal*.[3] He has also created the Julius Knipl radio cartoons, based on his most famous character. The radio cartoon version of the comic titled "The Radiator Musician" brings the absurd idea of its eponymous strip to life in an entertaining two minutes and forty seconds. Background sound effects clang and hiss while Katchor reads the strip's third-person narration. The words of the comic's minor characters are voiced by different actors in a theatrical style that recalls radio shows from the 1930s to the 1950s. The absurd dialogue of the radio clip is thus rendered as the auditory equivalent of the lived-in visual feel of the artist's diegetic world. It has even been suggested that these radio cartoons merit categorization as comics, despite lacking drawn images entirely.[4]

The strips and pages discussed in this chapter testify to the multivalent signifying properties of sound in Katchor's comics art. First up is "The Ringing Pay Phone (*BSD*, 18), a comic where one urbanite takes it upon himself to act as sympathetic listener, thereby perhaps alleviating the collective alienation of the city's inhabitants. Next, "Euro Trash / American Garbage" (*HDA*, 58) plays with the idea of terroir, which is perhaps more easily recognized in the wine industry. In agricultural settings, the unique properties of a given soil work together with other place-bound conditions to give each crop of grapes used in wine making a distinct taste; in urban settings, Katchor would have readers know, the sounds made during a given city's trash collection service are similarly unique. Finally, two pages from *The Jew of*

New York (*JNY*, 32–33) delve into the more mystical connotations of sound as they have evolved in the practice of Kabbalah. This example also draws from the artist's interest in spoken language more generally.

The Sound of Loneliness

Unsurprisingly, Katchor has a fondness for landline telephones. "The Ringing Pay Phone" (*BSD*, 18) taps into a now-dated urban soundscape that is less likely to be remembered by Katchor's readers with each passing year. There was a time—in a world where cell phones were not ubiquitous, of course—when it was not uncommon to hear pay phones ringing on the streets. If you were lucky, there was one in a central location where your friends would congregate. You could call the number and see who was there. Of course, it might ring because of a wrong number. Someone picking up a ringing public phone might want for a bit of unexpected conversation. The spontaneity of urban life comes in many forms. Nowadays, the ringing of a pay phone is the auditory sign of a bygone technological world, and as such it suits Katchor's set of comics themes perfectly.

"The Ringing Pay Phone" in question appears in each of the strip's eight panels (fig. 2.1). On the comics page, it becomes a visual marker of the density of urban communities and a symbol of the complexity of urban communication networks. The perspective from which the phone is drawn shifts constantly throughout. Katchor shows it from a variety of angles. He places it in the foreground, midground, and background of the empaneled space. The liveliness of these compositional choices reflects the spontaneity of the urban experience in general and also conveys the character's own mild excitement. The strip is dynamic in another sense, too. In panels 2, 5, and 8, Katchor whites out the panel's background so that we see only the phone box and the main character grasping its receiver. Despite being surrounded by people and cars moving

Fig. 2.1. Ben Katchor, "The Ringing Pay Phone," in *The Beauty Supply District* (Pantheon Books, 2000), 18. Reprinted with the generous permission of Ben Katchor.

through the big city, he seems to be having a moment of relative privacy. Looking directly at readers, the character takes on the role of an urban correspondent. In panel 5, he holds the telephone receiver up and angles it toward us so that we can better hear the person speaking on its other end. He has a message for us.

But who is this man? And what message does he want to leave us with? In the second panel, the man tells one wrong-number caller that his name is Eugene Gumtrop. The choice fits in well with Katchor's preference for names that sound like food items. Despite the risible name choice, we are given to believe that he is a sincere man. His mild excitement in the strip comes from the fact that he is convinced he is performing a good deed. He is undeterred by the warnings that one should never answer a public pay phone: "We're taught from childhood not to—that no good can come of it," he says in the first panel. Instead he chooses to buck inherited tradition. He has become a part-time do-gooder who answers a specific phone on a regular basis. The strip is careful not to turn Gumtrop into a buffoon, but there is no shortage of pathetic humor in his meager ambition and misplaced benevolence. The narrator informs us that what we are witnessing occurs "five days a week, during a casual stroll to and from a favorite sandwich shop." Katchor often uses storefront signage as a playful way of underscoring the theme of a comic, and this strip is no exception. The man's favorite sandwich shop appears in the first panel and is called "Caritas," underscoring that he sees his strange behavior as a form of charity.

Elsewhere, Katchor has created comics that mythologize the mundane activities of urbanites, in a way sacralizing the city. For instance, the common washing machine is said to be performing "baptismal rites" (*CV*, 62) on our collective clothing: "Our most intimate possessions are thrown into a communal bath to be symbolically cleansed of all cultural associations." Staring into car windows is the domain not just of the petty thief but also of "the gifted seer" ("The Parked-Car Reader," *JK*, 29). "The Hall of Pedestrians" (*HDA*, 116) displays items imbued with transcendent historical significance such as "a walk / don't walk sign, Boston, c. 1980," "a decorative cast-iron bench from the avenue des champs-Élysées, c. 1850," and "an audio recording of high heels on a Los Angeles street, 1976." Someone named Muni Tymus becomes "the Patron Saint of Jaywalkers" (*BSD*, 45).

In "The Ringing Pay Phone," we appear to be the only witnesses to Eugene Gumtrop's good deeds, and perhaps only we can judge whether he has both the patience and the humility to reach saintly status. He hears only the best in people ("Most are just innocent souls" / "I do my best to help them out—only a small percentage are up to no good"). We learn that he is humble. After losing his patience with a caller in panel 7, he apologizes to us in panel 8. He is well aware that his work brings him into contact with the seedy strata of urban life. In the third panel, he admits that "the soiled receivers, the unbathed strangers on the other end of the line are not pleasant." Perhaps his perseverance despite such difficulties ingratiates him to us.

If the "Twelve-Noon Siren" (*JK*, 57) had a "plaintive cry," the sound of the phone ringing appears to be just as emotionally resonant for Katchor. In a strip from *Cheap Novelties*, it is the middle of the night, and Julius Knipl is "half awakened by a fragmentary ring of his telephone" (*CN*, 79). The sound induces in the half-conscious Knipl a series of five thought-images that run a full emotional range. He experiences hunger ("an open salami on his kitchen table begins to sweat"), anxiety ("two men, who owe him money, sit in an all-night delicatessen and renew their pledge to never pay"), newfound curiosity ("a formerly unappealing toothpick dispenser now beckons him"), tragic indignity ("a truck backs onto his mother's grave"), and the banality of living ("he realizes that he's gone through a lifetime's supply of paper bags in just forty years"). The narrative form of this strip bears some similarity with the aforementioned comic about the sound of a man's cough, which appears just two pages earlier in the same collection (*CN*, 77). In each case, a different sound sends Knipl's mind racing. Here the tone is more humorous than tragic.

As if Eugene Gumtrop were himself a reader of Katchor's comics, the main character of "The Ringing Pay Phone" understands that modern urban life is riven with alienation. Individual city dwellers feel alone in their troubles, unconnected from the urban multitude. In their misdialed numbers, an attentive listener hears a cry for connection. In the final panel, the narrator gives voice to Gumtrop's deeper motivation: "There is no such thing as a wrong number." There is an intentionality on Gumtrop's part to perform his urban charity work. He has a sincere need to do his part to assuage the toll of urban alienation. This sincerity makes him at once a tragic and humorous figure, two qualities that one often finds together in Katchor's strips.

Sonic Terroir

Although the full-page color strip "Euro Trash / American Garbage" (*HDA*, 58) pokes fun at both supposed European refinement and American consumerism, its focus on urban noise presents commonalities with Katchor's other comics. In the city, unbearable noises are everywhere, and one must either put them to positive use or eradicate them entirely. On the one hand, for example, in "What Bruno Yule Heard" (*HDA*, 34–35), an entrepreneur attempts to market loud noises to consumers and residents in various ways; and in "The Eustachian Restaurant" (*HDA*, 139), loud noise allows diners to enjoy their meal without intruding thoughts. On the other hand, in "The Current Occupant" (*HDA*, 41), an apartment dweller is judged to be too loud and must "affect a late 19th century middle-class demeanor. . . . [and] wear carpet slippers and walk in a less obstreperous manner." Initially he is referred to "a psychologist who specializes in architectural incompatibility." Later he is evicted, and when he refuses to leave his residence, he is interned in a detention center.

"Euro Trash / American Garbage" is organized into two vertical stories that correspond with the two halves of its compound title.

Each vertical story consists of four rows of two panels. Katchor's use of color is purposeful. Just as in "Passing Through" (*HDA*, 152; see chap. 1), here the use of two different palettes differentiates a cleansed and tidy space, in yellow and blue, from a grungy and emotionally charged space, in red and purple. A corresponding lexical contrast is contained in the title. Only Ben Katchor could suggest that "trash" is an upscale, elegant, European word and equate "garbage" with the dirt and grime of America.

The story on the left carries the reader through scenes of trash collection in a range of global European cities (fig. 2.2). The final panels help to frame what comes before. A man declares his confidence in quite an unexpected skill: he can recognize the geographic location of any trash pickup just by hearing its sound. "Blindfold me, take me anywhere in the world and allow me to listen." As readers cross the gutter between the penultimate and the final panel, they realize that this is exactly what has happened. Standing on the second floor of a hotel in the Catalonian capital, he is able to correctly identify the "Ppaalachichahaca" sound emanating from the vehicle on the street below. Now in front of two witnesses, he states with great confidence: "Barcelona. That was easy."

In effect, the strip blends two forms of knowledge, taken from the musical and the culinary arts, and applies them in an absurd fusion. In the jazz world, during a time, so-called blindfold tests were held live on radio shows, or else their results were published in magazines. The idea was that listeners should be able to identify the unique sound produced by a jazz performer without knowing in advance which artist, album, or track they would be hearing. The other form of knowledge, of course, is taken from the importance of terroir in the wine industry. It is the uniqueness of a sonic jazz signature and of a wine's taste profile that makes it valuable. Persons knowledgeable in one or both of these areas are seen to possess signs of cultural distinction. The humor of Katchor's strip is produced by a debasement of this distinction, as he transposes such knowledge from a high to a low cultural form. And perhaps nothing could be lower status than the trash bin.

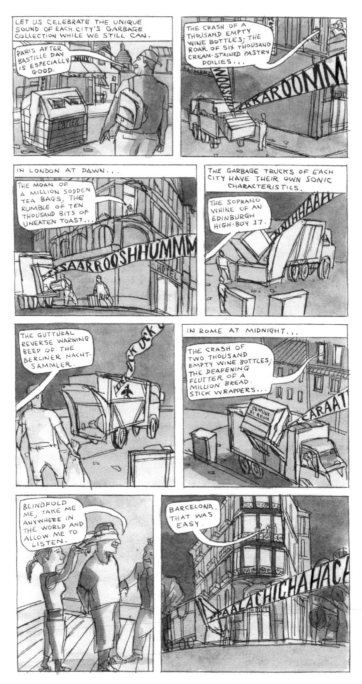

Fig. 2.2a. Ben Katchor, panels from the left half of "Euro Trash / American Garbage," in *Hand-Drying in America* (Pantheon Books, 2013), 58. Reprinted with the generous permission of Ben Katchor.

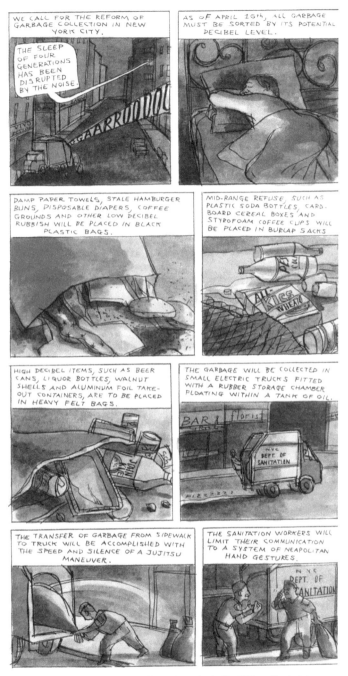

Fig. 2.2b. Ben Katchor, panels from the right half of "Euro Trash / American Garbage," in *Hand-Drying in America* (Pantheon Books, 2013), 58. Reprinted with the generous permission of Ben Katchor.

Even the sound of garbage offers potential raw material for a claim to privilege and refinement. As the narrator proposes in the first panel, "Let us celebrate the unique sound of each city's garbage while we still can." This language implies both the kind of scarcity that brings value to products on the market, and also the disappearance of a venerable and privileged way of life that is being corrupted by its popularity. Those with sufficient experience and a cultivated aural palette are well attuned to the unique sounds of urban refuse. Thus, in Paris, one hears "the crash of a thousand empty wine bottles; the roar of six thousand cream-stained pastry doilies"; in London, "the moan of a million sodden tea bags, the rumble of ten thousand bits of uneaten toast." The refined urbanite should surely be able to distinguish between the "sonic characteristics" of different garbage trucks. There are differences of pitch and timbre between "the soprano whine of an Edinburgh High-Boy 17" and "the guttural reverse warning beep of the Berliner Nacht-Sammler," for example. In the European context, at least, there is an intellectual enjoyment and a form of cultural distinction in being able to recognize the "kkarooom," the "sssaarrooshhumm," the "nnihhaaa," the "uck uck uck," and the "ccaraattt" of trash collection.

By comparison with Europe, America is home to a most crass form of garbage collection. Substituting the sounds of urban trash collection for images of refuse, Katchor doubles down on the fundamental cultural contrast of his strip. Close-up depictions of identifiable pieces of garbage—such as hamburger buns, bottles, and cans, and an "All-Kics Wheat" cereal box—bring readers into close contact with trash. No longer the object of contemplation, garbage assumes the status of a public menace. The strip's first panel urgently emphasizes the need for social change: "We call for the reform of garbage collection in New York City." The American system is out of balance. The heavy-handed approach of the reformers seeks to remove as much noise from the activity of garbage collection as possible. Sorting garbage "by its potential decibel level" into either plastic bags, burlap sacks, or heavy felt bags will lessen the impact on urbanites. As an additional sonic precaution, trash collectors will drive electronic vehicles and use hand gestures in lieu of speech. The comic hints that they will receive training to transfer trash into the truck more quietly. The goal is that the task "be accomplished with the speed and silence of a jujitsu maneuver."

Clearly the humor of the strip's absurd idea comes from entrenched ideas about Americans and Europeans. Yet this obvious geographic contrast also has a subtle temporal dimension. In the words spoken by the European side's narrator—the "while we still can"—one hears an anxiety: an unrefined global culture fueled by America's crass consumerism is, unfortunately, having an impact even across the Atlantic.

Mystical Onomatopoeia

There can be no doubt that Katchor is fascinated by language. In interviews, he has indicated that his ideas for comics generally start with a script, thus with the words, and the breakdown into paneled images comes afterward.[5] His interest in language pushes beyond English to Yiddish, Hebrew, and invented tongues as well. He has a propensity for wordplay but combines this playfulness with more conceptual ideas or esoteric topics.

As we have seen, he gives often silly, but still highly evocative, names to his characters (e.g., Gallstone, Salamis, Gumtrop). And one always needs to look closely at his fictitious storefronts (e.g., Caritas). A perfect example of this is the first comic collected in *Julius Knipl, Real Estate Photographer* ("The Drowned Men's Association," *JK*, 1–4), which features two different views of a certain "Tsimtsum Industries" building. The word *tsimtsum* in its modern usage comes from the kabbalistic thought of Isaac Luria and "means briefly that the existence of the universe is made possible by a process of shrinkage in God."[6] More learned readers of the strip can thus also assess the possible thematic connection between a divine withdrawal from the world and the impending bankruptcy of Tsimtsum Industries Inc.

Words borrowed from Yiddish are not infrequent in Katchor's strips. Particularly common are those relating to food (e.g., "knishes," *JK*, 1; "a shmir of mustard," *CN*, 85; cheese blintzes, *DR*, 494). One of the full-page illustrations from *The Dairy Restaurant* presents a table spread with various Ashkenazic Jewish dairy-based foods, as Katchor contrasts milkhiker (dairy) and fleyshiker (meat) cuisines: knishes, blintzes, vernitshkes, kneydlekh, and the like (*DR*, 142). Readers will also see words unrelated to food, like "shpotzir" (*JK*, 40), which refers to a stroll with no destination taken by the title character of "The Escalator Rider" (*JK*, 40). Both transliterated Hebrew and Yiddish appear in *The Jew of New York* (e.g., Mr. Marah says both "Ribbono shel olam" and "Avade, ikh ken a bisl Yidish"; *JNY*, 19, 92). In *The Dairy Restaurant*, Katchor also includes a variety of advertisements in Yiddish, written with the Hebrew alphabet.

The graphic novel version of *The Jew of New York* prominently features Hebrew lettering on its cover, where the title is written out as דה׳ דזשו אוו נ׳ו ׳ארק. In this usage, Hebrew letters suggest the English words and pronunciation. One particular segment contained in the volume provides insight into the origin of this idea. The character Nathan Kishon stumbles upon a "communistic sect founded upon the scientific principles of the great genius and discoverer of oxygen, Joseph Priestly" (*JNY*, 27–30). Kishon is surprised to see the commune's name "spelt phonetically with Hebrew characters!" (27). While on a tour of the commune grounds, he gains knowledge of some of the sect's more absurd practices, but he also learns of an idea that seems somewhat less absurd. When he later tells Mr. Marah of his experience, the latter exclaims, "Judeo-German, Judeo-Spanish . . . why not, in time, a Judeo-American?" (28).[7] At the sect, we see a copy of the Declaration of Independence, written in English but using the Hebrew alphabet, whose transliterated title is דעקלער׳׳שאן אוו א׳נד׳פענדע נס דה׳ (28). Kishon's tour guide explains that the sect hopes "someday to see all American printing and writing done in Hebrew characters—only then can an indigenous language develop; only then will our severance from English culture be complete!" (28).

Katchor's interest in language spans both real and invented tongues. For example, *The Cardboard Valise* includes a detailed description of an all-but-forgotten language spoken by only a few inhabitants of Tensint Island: "Our language, if you can call a bastard jargon of double Dutch, pidgin English and salesmen's argot a language, developed from an earlier, unwritten birdlike song in the 1960s" (*CV*, 10). His comics are equally concerned not merely with how words read but also with how they sound. The character in this example rattles off a list of a few of the words that "have been incorporated into our daily speech. 'Norlazik': a shoelace that's come undone by itself; 'sapajuliast': a monkey with a technical skill; 'tsatskatchewon': a lost toy; 'aeturnapy': a frozen hamburger that will never be defrosted" (*CV*, 10). Here, as elsewhere in the collection, we encounter Katchor as amateur linguist who is quite passionate about serious wordplay. Later, for instance, he explains the Forfesque system, a manner of speaking efficiently, which "has simply reduced all words by one or more syllables and then linked them together, wherever possible, in common pairs; long vowels are converted to short ones, un-necessary consonants discarded" (*CV*, 70).

It is in *The Jew of New York* that Katchor most humorously indulges the absurdity of connections between language and sound (*JNY*, 32–33; see figs. 2.3, 2.4). His decision to fashion the character of Yosl Feinbroyt as a kabbalist brings up a host of historical and religious associations. Those who may know very little of Kabbalah may certainly still enjoy this segment's deep dive into the transcendent sound of a belch. Still, the specificity of Katchor's text and images undoubtedly adds to this humor by alluding to the rich history of kabbalist practice.

It is significant that when Feinbroyt is first introduced, it is as "a latter-day disciple of the famous kabbalist and vagrant, Abraham Abulafia" (*JNY*, 32). As depicted by Katchor, Feinbroyt's activities are indeed a humorous echo of the historical Abulafia's own brand of practical mysticism.[8] Kabbalah is a diverse set of thought and practices, but one branch promises the mystic direct knowledge of God through various meditative methods. This was a hidden form of knowledge passed down from teacher to student, of which relatively few written texts survived.[9] Kabbalah is at once "deeply conservative and intensely revolutionary." Abulafia himself was highly innovative. His emphasis on divine revelation brought him a certain amount of notoriety both as "the outstanding representative of ecstatic Kabbalism" and also as "the least popular of all the great Kabbalists." In particular, his emphasis on individual mystical experience is what alienated him from the more orthodox kabbalists of his time. Abulafia's lack of popularity in a sense makes him a perfect choice for Katchor's comics, where vagrants, drifters, outsiders, and the urban periphery loom large.

When we first meet Yosl Feinbroyt, he is spending a typical afternoon in the café known as the Chaldean Gardens (fig. 2.3). He is listening intently to the sounds created by the other patrons around him who are eating and drinking. We see him inscribe the onomatopoeic words "zhaloup" and "choup" in a book as others in the café make noises like "gluk" and "grepts." While the images and word balloons largely show us the activities, conversations, and eructations of the surrounding patrons, the narration conveys the mystical significance of Feinbroyt's activities. In all four panels of the bottom row in the verso strip, the narration seems to be a series of quotations taken from a book on mystical meditation, perhaps one written by Abraham Abulafia himself: "Now begin to combine a few or many letters, to permute them and to combine them until thy heart be warm." As recorded in the Sefer Yetzirah, an early kabbalistic text known to Abraham Abulafia, the meditative permutation and combination of letters is one of the methods for seeking divine knowledge. Feinbroyt's list of belch vocabulary is being framed by the narrator as an offshoot of just this branch of individual mystical pursuit.

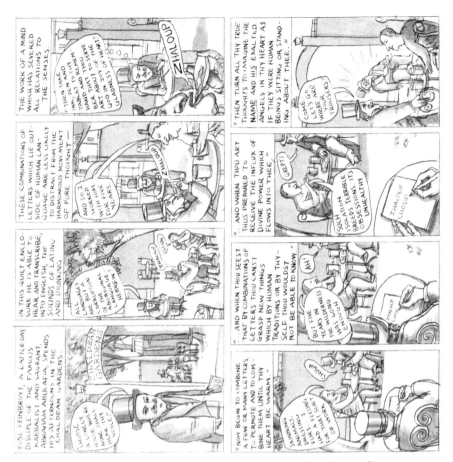

Fig. 2.3. Ben Katchor, "Yosl Feinbroyt, Latter-Day Kabbalist," in *The Jew of New York* (Pantheon Books, 1998), 32. Reprinted with the generous permission of Ben Katchor.

In the last panel of the verso strip, Katchor draws—quite uncharacteristically, in the context of his larger oeuvre, at least—a number of bright rays emanating from Yosl Feinbroyt's body. It is as if the character has reached a meditative state of ecstasy through his contemplation of belch onomatopoeia. With his arms slack and his head tilted to one side, Feinbroyt is also asnooze. Katchor's strip implicitly poses a provocative and humorous question: is there a difference? In the recto strip, one of the servers at the Chaldean Gardens tells his coworker, "He comes here every day in an ecstatic trance," highlighting once again the character's resonance with Abulafia's ecstatic pursuit of divine knowledge (fig. 2.4).

The visual narration also carries this story of mystical revelation forward with images that readers must presume are what Feinbroyt sees in his mind's eye. Text and image work in tandem, presenting readers with a journey described in the book of Ezekiel and kept alive in throne mysticism and the Merkabah tradition.[10] Our latter-day kabbalist bounds up a "luminous" staircase, walks through "palatial hall," and stops at a "delicate curtain," on which is embroidered a single word. Engraved on the stairs are words such as "zhaloup," "choup," "gluk," "chalop," "shump." Feinbroyt's progression up the steps and movement through the palatial architecture serve as an allegory for deepening mystical knowledge of God. The intense light and the slivers of shadow cast by columns in the hall connote architectural grandeur but also divine splendor. The final embroidered word is written in both Hebrew and Latin letters: "גרעפץ/grepts." It is "a crude, onomatopoeic representation of the eternal sound of relief." Katchor has elevated the common belch to the status of a transcendent pathway to knowledge of the divine.

The gravitas of this representation of mystical experience is undercut in two ways—first, by the two panels where Feinbroyt is fast asleep, arms dangling and head cocked; second, by the debasement of the pretensions to enlightenment, the fact that a higher state might be reached through contemplation of such a crude bodily noise. The episode may be a send-up of Kabbalah's

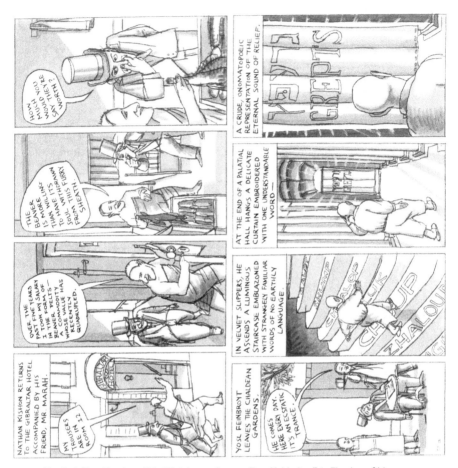

Fig. 2.4. Ben Katchor, "Yosl Feinbroyt, Latter-Day Kabbalist," in *The Jew of New York* (Pantheon Books, 1998), 33. Reprinted with the generous permission of Ben Katchor.

pretensions to mystical understanding, and perhaps also of obsessive thinking in general; but in another way, it is also a celebration of embodiment. The humor of the comic comes from the contrast between the body and the mind, the bodily here and now versus the transcendent world beyond our sight. One thing is certain: whether the sound of a belch is the vehicle that makes transcendence possible, or whether it simply connotes digestive relief as it slips out over the dining table, sounds have the power to move us, and to make us laugh.[11]

CHAPTER 3

Touch

With the rise of e-books, digital platforms, web comics, and the like, it would be easy to conclude that tactility—the tangible book we hold in our hands—is less and less a part of the modern reading experience. This is perhaps an overstatement, as the consumption of digital media also entails its own kind of material experience. Still, the role that touch plays in the experience of reading print materials is commonsensical. The book is a material object in its own right.

The material book is also a symbol of sorts. It stands in for an entire print culture. To hold a novel, a guidebook, or a comic in one's hand is to feel the weight of a much larger industrial manufacturing chain. Books have a life cycle of their own. Touch is implicated throughout the publishing process. There is the labor involved in sourcing raw materials, and in the physical efforts involved in book production, packaging, distribution, and shelving for sale. After a book is purchased, a brief period of use is likely to be quickly followed by a longer period of neglect. While some books become highly coveted possessions and are passed down from one generation to the next (see fig. 1.2 and the discussion of "Jubilation Alley" in chap. 1), others are acquired by a rotating cast of emotionally unavailable owners, destined to spend most of their lives at the bottom of a forgotten box. At the end of the life cycle lies the great remaindering process. Books are deemed unfit for sale. All flesh is grass; all pages are pulp. There is something Katchorean about the very idea of it.

Tactility is involved in many ways in the experience of reading a book. As Ian Hague suggests, one must attend to both physical properties and performative practices. There are properties like "texture, material composition, hardness, flexibility, weight and temperature" to consider, just as there are practices that are "culturally determined and relatively conventional (e.g., the turning of pages)."[1] Ben Katchor's print comics can be highly attuned to this notion of the book as a material object. In "The Corner Location" (introduction; see fig. I.3–4), for example, he integrates the fold of the printed page into the comic's diegesis. Touch is important as a represented theme in his comics art as well. In "Jubilation Alley," Julius Knipl helps a stranger by picking up pieces of the pages of a treasured novel that have fallen onto the floor of the subway car (fig. 1.2).

Touch is also implicated as readers first open a book, as they handle its paratextual zones. Generally speaking, these zones do not exist in comics in the same way as they do in prose books.[2] That is, whereas in prose publishing the cover, title page, foreword, afterword, chapter title pages, margins, and the like are seen as external to the story—as part of an additional editorial aesthetic or marketing strategy—these elements form an integral part of the storytelling in comics. Katchor's creations exploit this quality of comics to the maximum. Both *Hand-Drying in America* and *The Cardboard Valise* use the inside front and back covers, as well as front and back matter pages, as canvases for still more comics storytelling. The oversize dimensions of *Hand-Drying in America*—11.75 inches wide by 12.25 inches tall—draw marked attention to the physicality of the book. Its cover image serves as the first panel of a comics story that ends on the back cover. As designed by Chip Kidd, the cover of *The Cardboard Valise* has two handles that fold outward, making it possible for someone to carry the collection as if it were a piece of luggage. Depictions of invented historical documents interrupt the reading of *The Jew of New York* in its collected graphic novel form, and real menus from New York restaurants dot the later pages of *The Dairy Restaurant*. Both of these collections also begin the comics storytelling on the inside covers, the latter with an image of a "primordial borscht" (priced at 75 cents a bowl), accompanied by a verse from the first book of the Pentateuch (Genesis/בראשית 1:2).

The 2016 edition of *Cheap Novelties* is also notable in this regard. Its front and back inside covers are home to invented advertisements in red newsprint, and the exterior covers feature news stories and even another Katchor comic in yellowing newspaper. This newspaper appears to be wrapped around the edges of the book. Neatly folded and affixed on the interior, its presence alludes to a do-it-yourself culture—that is, some of us may still remember making homemade paper covers to protect an important book from damage. The comic is situated on a vertical fold of the back cover. In it, Julius Knipl is unable to stop himself from reading gimmick newspapers that are published in a print run of one. Reading is an acquired impulse, and the ubiquity of print reading materials in the modern city makes its use compulsory.

Part of what makes newspapers, books, historical documents, restaurant menus, and other cheap novelties so appealing is the way they feel. Objects stimulate our sense of touch. Through that sense, they appeal to our emotions, our memories, and the ideas we have about ourselves. Though he would have us know he is not a "serious or systematic collector" of objects, Katchor himself makes an interesting admission: "I used to collect matchbox labels. . . . They were made all over the world. My favorites are from India."[3] The idea that tactility is gratifying is self-evident in his comics. But through this single idea, he leads us down a number of different paths.

This chapter uses the idea of touch and tactility to explore different themes in Katchor's comics storytelling. As discussed in the example of "The Kozma Theater" (chap. 1; see fig. 1.1), tactile objects are threaded throughout the Julius Knipl strips collected in *Cheap Novelties*, where they are given prominent placement in the upper-left panel of each comic. No exception to this principle, the strip titled "An Eccentric Dry Cleaner" (*CN*, 69) zeroes in on those small material objects that one picks up in the course of an urban life, and that are easily forgotten in the pockets of garments. "On the Newsstand" (*HDA*, 20), one of the comics included in *Hand-Drying in America*, is concerned with the unique architectural properties of street kiosks, but also with the wider culture of print that sustains these outposts of the literate metropolis. Finally, several strips from *The Cardboard Valise* deal with the book-manufacturing process, the life cycle of books, and the demise of print culture. The innovative design of the collection's physical form highlights the rarefaction to which the book as material object has been subjected in the twenty-first century.

Tactile Memory

There can be no doubt about Katchor's fondness for the object world: "With great acuity he probes how humans interact with objects—especially those discarded and lain to waste."[4] The mere sight of an object is enough to induce a certain reaction. In "The Cheap Merchandise District" (*CN*, 93–109, 105), a long-form comic published at the end of the *Cheap Novelties* re-release, Katchor's character Moishe Nustril meditates on bodily responses to visual stimuli. The editorial that Nustril is writing assumes that "the terrible struggle for economic survival" leaves urbanites in a "weakened condition." In such a state, "the sight of any glittering object—a new key chain, the polished finial atop a building or the eye of a loved one—is enough to stimulate the medulla of the suprarenal gland [adrenal gland]." It is the conditioning of the market economy that explains "the physiological basis of man's insatiable acquisitiveness" and, as Nustril goes on to say, "haphazard production and unequal distribution of wealth." Sight appeals to our baser motives, prompting a culture of acquisitiveness and accumulation. Vision can precede touch in this way.

For its part, touch can appeal to visual memories that do not always align with our immediate surroundings. "An Eccentric Dry Cleaner" (*CN*, 69) suggests that a powerful link exists between touch and memory. Tangible objects seem to carry their own sense memories along with them. The strip's textual and visual narration may cause readers to ponder the power of tactile memory. We may wonder whether it is possible to remember experiences that are not in fact our own. The strip begins with an unnamed dry cleaner who speaks aloud as he works, more for our benefit than for that of any given customer: "When a garment comes in to be cleaned, I'm careful to empty the pockets. / Ticket stubs, bus transfers, invitations, toothpicks . . . I don't throw anything away." Rather than collect these discarded items, he in fact repurposes them: "After the garment's nice and clean, I try my best to put something back into every pocket." It is not wholly satisfying to see this dry cleaner as a simple trickster. Rather, he seems cut from the same cloth as Eugene Gumtrop in "The Ringing Pay Phone" (chap. 2; see fig. 2.1). This is low-impact altruism at its best, carried out at the urban margins. The dry cleaner simply hopes to share the pleasure he finds in forgotten objects with his customers.

The cheap novelty Katchor chooses for this strip's upper-left panel is a pushpin. For those who can imagine finding this object in their pocket, there may be a visual-tactile metaphor in play, something along the lines of the pinprick of memory. The Julius Knipl pushpin works as a condensed representation of the ties that govern tactility and emotion, body, and mind.

The diegetic world of this nine-panel, two-row strip is at once more narrow and more expansive than other Julius Knipl strips (fig. 3.1). That is, there is a sense of confinement conveyed by the comic's central mental image: a dry cleaner who rummages around in the pockets of garments. Also contributing to this sense of enclosure is the fact that panels 1, 2, and 5 depict the interior of the business. In the first two panels, one cannot even make out the name of the store, whose reverse lettering on the street-facing window is covered up by word balloons ("Dr——Cleane——"). Knowledge of the location is frustrated again in panel 5, where readers can only see part of the clothes hanger's logo ("Clean——"). Yet these interior views are juxtaposed with the exteriors of panels 3 and 4, where Knipl strolls along a street, holding a memento

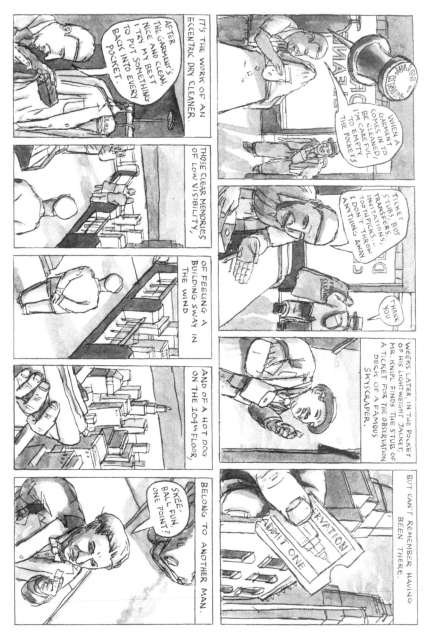

Fig. 3.1. Ben Katchor, "An Eccentric Dry Cleaner," in *Cheap Novelties* (Drawn & Quarterly, 2016), 69. Reprinted with the generous permission of Ben Katchor.

found in his coat pocket. Here, the low-angle perspective of panel 3, which shows us the sky above the city, seems to mirror the lofty considerations of its central character and the more expansive mindset of the strip's narrator.

Knipl has in his hand "the stub of a ticket for the observation deck of a famous skyscraper" (text from panel 3), which subsequently appears in close-up (image from panel 4). Together, text and image anticipate the skyscraper views in panels 6, 7, and 8. These views, however, simply do not display any experience that Knipl might have had. Regarding the skyscraper, the narrator informs us that Knipl "can't remember having been there." Still, the visual and textual narration of these three panels allow us a glimpse into "those clear memories of low visibility, / of feeling a building sway in the wind / and of a hot dog on the 104th floor." Other people are present on the skyscraper's observation deck, though not a face can be seen. Their relationship to the specific space and time of the comic's story is left vague. Along with the narrator, we see what Knipl cannot: the memories "of another man." It is unclear whether the person appearing in the comic's last panel is this other man, or someone else altogether. Either way, his expressed confusion at the object found in his own pocket ("Skee-ball fun, one point?") carries a message: the eccentric dry cleaner's work of memory regifting will continue.

Katchor's comic affirms the innate value of lost and discarded objects but simultaneously concludes that this value cannot be retrieved. The mere touch of these objects may have the ability to prompt memories of a past experience, but it appears that only the third-person narrator has the ability to access them. The wording of the narration ("those clear memories") in panel 5 suggests the existence of some sort of urban memory repository, some sort of collating urban consciousness that can archive and point to the specific memories in question. The use of the demonstrative adjective implies a contrast (i.e., "those" memories, not "these memories"). They are out there, or up there, floating above the city. But a chasm separates memory from tactile stimulus, a chasm that is recapitulated in the disjunction established between the street level and the skyscraper views in the strip. A similar chasm exists between urbanites who are alienated from one another. The chances that any two of the dry cleaner's customers will ever meet to swap objects is slim to none.

Print Culture

For Katchor, printed materials are among the most precious of tactile objects. In interviews, he has discussed the materiality of comics:

> Cheap printing, bleeding of ink on absorbent newsprint, off-register color, etc. were all part of the material charm of comics in newspapers and comic books. These qualities were the result of a publisher cutting costs, not someone consciously exploiting the qualities of newsprint, but the result is the same.[5]

He has also stressed that the materiality of comics can be quite limiting: "Comics have this kind of material specificity. They're made for a certain size and to do other things with them is always another design problem."[6] In this material specificity, the artist perceives a twinge of tragedy.

To wit, his strip titled "The Tragic History of the Oversized Magazine" (*HDA*, 90–91) offers a veritable history of print publishing in the tragic mode. He depicts the broadsheets that were read in eighteenth-century coffeehouses in London and mentions the perfection of the halftone process in the late nineteenth century. The strip ends with the illustrated magazine industry of the twentieth century, whose peak may very well have been during the 1970s and '80s. After covering everything from lithography to printing plants and large rotary presses with a triumphant tone, the narration suddenly turns sour. The increasing price of paper and the "dawn of electronic publishing" force a shift in the oversize magazine's readership. Something that was once popular has become elite, rarified.

The comic titled "On the Newsstand" (*HDA*, 20) takes place at a time and a place marked by the beginnings of this turn away from print culture (fig. 3.2). As the narration in panel 5 informs us, "We have arrived at the last stop on the well-worn track of 19th-century printing and distribution." The strip's tone is more celebratory than tragic, however. In essence, we have here a clear visual ode to the common news kiosk. By extension, this is at once an ode to the thriving print culture that sustained it.

Katchor gives the stand a name with positive connotations, "Enthrall News," and bathes the panels with warm colors. The yellow glow of artificial lighting is used throughout and contrasts with the cold grayish blue of the urban night and its shadows. We follow an unnamed protagonist as he exits the brightly lit lobby of his apartment building in search of reading material. The bulb lighting of the "Enthrall News" kiosk illuminates the dark street, creating a cozy refuge. By foregrounding this contrast of coloring and lighting, panels 2, 3, 6, and 7 depict the newsstand as a sort of urban beacon for lovers of print.

Ostensibly, the comic is centered on the newsstand's architecture. The textual narration's matter-of-fact tone emphasizes the kiosk's rudimentary construction: "The point of purchase is a three-dimensional structure with a particular door, window and roof." It boasts an economical design whose practical benefits have become more marked during a period of decline in print reading. "The fashion magazines, newspapers and journals of culture are reduced to a form an insulation"; they have become mere "paper shingles." Nonetheless, framed by its wide, open, welcoming doors, the newsstand refuses to be cowed by a downturn in print readership. This "crude shelter" may be the "last stop" on the road of print culture, but it has a certain dignity nonetheless.

Color is the primary vehicle for Katchor's celebration of the dignity of this waning culture. He complements the warm yellow light emanating from the kiosk by using a rich red for its exterior and

Fig. 3.2. Ben Katchor, "On the Newsstand," in *Hand-Drying in America* (Pantheon Books, 2013), 20. Reprinted with the generous permission of Ben Katchor.

signage. Similarly, the nameless "man who sits inside" the newsstand, who is visible in five of the strip's nine panels, also wears a bright red shirt. The final two panels carry these color choices further. Having retreated to the cozy interior of his apartment, the protagonist-purchaser has changed his clothing. The cold colors of his street clothes have now been replaced by yellow pajamas. The warm red of his couch upholstery echoes the reds of the kiosk panels. A compositional inversion has occurred here. Whereas the red figure of the kiosk employee was surrounded by a warm yellow glow (panel 5), the protagonist's yellow figure is bordered by the red couch material (panel 8) on which he relaxes. The effect conveyed by color in these complementary panels is to emphasize the kiosk and the apartment as two nodes in one larger system.

In this sense, the comic's title is pulling double duty. "On the Newsstand" signals the location of the printed magazine, which the protagonist has purchased for $3.95. But it also delivers the strip into a mode of historical explication, offering information "on," "about," or "regarding" the newsstand. The last panel features an exterior view where a warm yellow glow emanates from both the lobby of the comfy reader's building and his fifth-story window. The social importance of print culture lies in the tactile pleasure of flipping through a magazine's pages, but also in the conversation the protagonist has at the point of purchase. As the first panel's narration explains, "A subscription by email is not the same." The conversation at the kiosk may be unremarkable, but its glow nevertheless follows the protagonist home and enlivens his solitary reading. While flipping the pages of his recently purchased magazine on his couch, the protagonist develops sympathy for the kiosk employee. His thoughts are meant to evoke our own: "Alone, at home, with our magazine, we think for a moment of what it would be like to sit in that narrow stall, unable to turn around." The message is that what characterizes print culture is not just a certain form of reading but a network of sympathetic, social bonds.

Elsewhere, Katchor deals even more directly with the rise-and-fall narrative of print culture. A strip that he published later in

Metropolis titled "The Last Stand" (*HDA*, 138) humorously illustrates the unwanted effects of this downturn. "With the demise of print publishing . . . / the city's newsstands turn to the sale of other merchandise"—such as lip balm and pocket-size packages of tissue. The largest panel of this strip features a callback to "On the Newsstand," too. Customers of "the last stand" make comments like "The cold of winter without insulation" and "These empty racks are freezing." Without print media lining the shelves, the newsstand no longer has any physical insulation. Everyone is now more exposed to the elements. The cold blue wash of this panel emphasizes not merely the cold temperatures but also a collective emotional response to the loss of print culture. We spend our days "immersed in a reality of pixels" and still long for human connection.

The Life Cycle of Books

An anecdote from Katchor's professional life in 1995 provides a striking image. It centers on a material artifact from a tactile culture of print that one, paradoxically, cannot touch:

> I was between newspapers for a year or so. Nobody in New York could see my weekly strip, so I built these Plexiglas cases with a fluorescent light at the top and a board in the middle. Two big, blown-up images of my strips could be put on either side—this week's strip and last week's. One was in the window of the B&H Dairy, and one was at a Papaya King on 86th and Lexington, on the Upper East Side. The idea was that you could go there and read the strip in the street. Because this was before the internet, there was no other way to get things to people.[7]

Readers who want to see what this might have looked like can turn to the strip "Accumulated Savings" (*BSD*, 15). In the background of its final panel, someone is reading an eight-panel comic strip. It is enclosed in an illuminated box in the window of what appears to be the Papaya King, thus closely matching Katchor's description. In the panel's foreground, a CPA named Jacob Rhesus comments on "the weekly exhibition of an obscure comic strip in the window of a late-night tropical drink stand" as he considers several extravagant but wasteful ways customers might spend their money.

The justification for this sort of public-facing display case is quite reasonable. Yet, as revealed by Katchor's own self-deprecating treatment of the event, there is also something curious about it. In retrospect, what is most striking is the idea that an object of tactile print culture—a comic strip whose natural habitat would be the folds of a popular weekly—should be so enclosed and thus rendered untouchable. There is in this image a metaphor for the rarefaction of print. This is print culture as a museum object—in a word, moribund.

No small portion of Katchor's work is concerned with what the demise of print culture looks like in practical terms. For example, what value do books have if they are not being read? This is a central question posed by several of the strips collected in *The Cardboard Valise* (2011). This book, which the artist has described as "a graphic novel in the form of a weekly comic strip," consists mainly of "a series of imaginary travelogues that explored the relativity of cultures, the power of the souvenir and the lure of things foreign."[8] But the theme of the book as a remnant of a bygone material culture also looms large. In one strip, "A hundred thousand copies of a guide-book are dropped from an airplane onto Tensint Island / Unsold copies of last year's edition" (*CV*, 17). Books are ballast, the residue of print culture, future pulp. In another strip, two alienated bibliophiles improbably meet while throwing away their paper trash, and one proposes a night on the town: "We'll compare definitions, have a few drinks and maybe, if we're lucky, pick up some cheap remaindered books" (*CV*, 72).

Most important, the collection gets its name from a multi-page strip about a cheap piece of luggage: "It's a new valise, but a cheap one," says a young traveler. "I wanted to see if it could withstand the rough handling of a large airport baggage system. / It's packed with a hundred pounds of old medical textbooks, back from when they were printed on that heavy coated paper" (*CV*, 1). The cardboard valise in this first comic of the volume is itself made from "pulp slurry": "It's a coarse grey cardboard speckled with an assortment of recycled scrap paper. / If you look closely, you'll see pieces of a pornographic magazine, Christmas wrapping paper and bloody tissue paper" (3). *The Cardboard Valise* collection is itself packaged in a way that keeps certain associations in the front of the minds of its readers—first, the luxury of travel, and second, the miserly connotations of inexpensive pulp.

The collection's design by Chip Kidd mimics the form of a suit-case. Two thin cardboard handles fold out from the front and back covers (figs. 3.3, 3.4). These are blue in color, which matches the blue sky in the scenes of Tensint Island depicted on the covers. They are an extension of the diegetic story space with which the collection begins. The island's name itself connotes cheap prices or knockoff goods (Tensint Island = a "ten-cent" island). Its claim to fame is that it is home to "the crumbling ruins of a once-great public restroom" (*CV*, 4). The cover images, together, form one continuous panoramic view of these majestic men's and women's restrooms, which have been carefully preserved as historical sites and marketed to foreigners as tourist destinations. The hues of the scene depicted on the cover are so strangely beautiful, and the cover design by Kidd is so sharp, that one can easily get lost in the book's materiality. On the back, there is even an aesthetic reminder of the idea that cheap materials that have been used in its construction. A noticeable tear surrounds the barcode and ISBN. The visual effect suggests that the cardboard has already begun to flake off the valise.

The front and back matter pages—including even the inside of the book's covers—are home to a comic of their own. In three double-page spreads, followed by three single-page images, Katchor offers a look into the life cycle of a book. The story starts with the felling of trees as the raw materials for pulp and

Fig 3.3. Ben Katchor, front cover of *The Cardboard Valise* (Pantheon Books, 2011). Reprinted with the generous permission of Ben Katchor.

Fig. 3.4. Ben Katchor, inside back cover of *The Cardboard Valise* (Pantheon Books, 2011). Reprinted with the generous permission of Ben Katchor.

ends just as "Friends and Family of the guidebook author Ishmael Jangle gather to watch as the unsold copies of his last book are remaindered." Floating in the penultimate panel is an image of the guidebook's cover. Its title references the restroom culture of Tensint Island with a bit of a wink, and the subtitle of this "final edition" announces its own irrelevance: "I Went on Tensint Island: A Discontinued History in One-and-a-Half Volumes."

Along the way, Katchor manages to eroticize quite a banal industry. There are "polygamous woodsmen" whose passion is ignited by the sound of chainsaws, and "avid readers [who] copulate in the shadow of the Nanchantz paper plant." In addition, inside the paper plant, "a new form of autoeroticism" develops: "To immediately relieve the pain of papercuts, the workers kiss their afflicted fingers," and "over an eight-hour shift, the crew becomes enervated and lovesick" (fig. 3.4). In Katchor's comic, the materiality and the tactility of books become intimately and comically linked to the sensuality of touch. He overemphasizes the connection by working through different registers: sexual urges, self-love, and romantic feelings. To wit, in another panel, "a printer in Gazogene city" checks the accuracy of coloring "in a small, self-published edition of love poems."[9]

Still, Ben Katchor would have us know that in reality all love fades or comes to an end. A full-page image of "discarded reference books" filling an entire industrial-size bin points to the immensity of these feelings driven by the collective experience of love lost. Through these emotive associations, readers come to recognize the fate of books as an allegory for the human condition. This story charting the life cycle of the book comes full circle in the comic's last panel on the inside back cover. At left, a mountain of paper spills from an enormous warehouse and connects to a waste-recycling machine. In the lower right of the image, someone's right hand holds up a portion of processed paper pulp for the reader's inspection. Is it the reader's own hand?[10] The effect is visceral. We are left with the thought that the destiny of all print is to be remaindered.[11]

This use of the front and back matter spaces of a collection to reflect on the life cycle of books is not unique to this travel-themed collection. *Hand-Drying in America* includes a comics story that is similar in both placement and theme. In contrast to the use of full-page illustrations in *The Cardboard Valise*, here the four front matter and two back matter pages are divided into eight or nine panels each. Once again, the designer of the material book is Chip Kidd. Katchor has stated explicitly that his use of endpaper comics in this case is intended as a metacommentary on book production.

> You have to have end papers in books, you know, and rather than putting a decorative pattern there I decided to kind of book-end the interior with this story. . . . I think there was [a need for] a strip specifically about the modern production of picture books, you know, these large size books. I could have boiled that down to a page too, but again the form and the context tell you what's possible. I wanted it to work both as end papers and as a story about contemporary book production.[12]

The strip actually begins on the front cover of *Hand-Drying in America* and ends on the back cover. It follows the character Josef Fuss from New York to China and back again. Though he is an investigative reporter, Fuss poses as a print buyer to visit a printing plant. The text zones of the comics are flooded with reminders that publishing is a for-profit industry. In one panel, the narration points out that "to realize a 15% corporate profit, it's necessary to reduce production costs." Exploitative labor practices abound. Employees catch a few moments of badly needed sleep on mats by the machines they operate, which "run 'round the clock." The stress causes one "despondent printer" to commit suicide by jumping off a roof.

Fuss is able to confirm what he likely suspected all along, that "each book is a minor ecological disaster."[13] One whole page of panels illustrates the fallout from consuming fossil fuels, releasing carbon dioxide and toxic runoff, producing acid rain, and depleting oxygen levels, all of it harming plant and animal life. Upon his return to the United States, Fuss publishes his exposé and grapples with both celebrity and criticism. In particular, "Lovers of books have difficulty accepting the report of Josef Fuss." While elsewhere in Katchor's oeuvre the materiality of book culture was coded in positive terms, here he shows his willingness to observe even print culture with a critical eye. In this new context, the book lover is revealed to be a snob who mistakes possession of books for possession of knowledge. "They were raised to believe that the mere ownership of particular books was a confirmation of one's intellect. / In fact, the smell and texture of paper is their last remaining physical pleasure" (*HDA*, title page).

On one of the collection's back matter pages, author Hiram Burro finishes "one last coffee-table" book of his lifetime and enjoys the "cool touch of coated paper" in his hands. But after reading the Fuss reports, Burro declares that "to go on, knowing what I now know, would be criminal!" As it was in "The Tragic History of the Oversized Magazine" (*HDA*, 90–91), print readership and the tactile media that sustain it are parts of a rarefied practice of the elite. As Katchor has said in an interview, "The thing is that the physicality of books makes them a kind of luxury—like driving a Cadillac. . . . It's a luxury to sell paperback books that require thirty gallons of water to produce. And they are disposable now—paperbacks are not things you necessarily will keep."[14] Still, as the image on the back cover of *Hand-Drying in America* reminds us, materiality is also the comfort of the analog masses: a New York street vendor spreads out a blanket of his wares on the city sidewalk. You may choose any print book you like for the low price of one dollar.

CHAPTER 4

Smell/Taste

B en Katchor is that rare comics artist whose pages capture not merely urban sights, sounds, and tactile sensations, but also the smells and tastes of city life. There is, in this full embrace of the human senses, a provocation of sorts. The "poetic logic" with which Katchor approaches the market economy recalls the poetic impulse of Walter Benjamin's Arcades Project. The suggestion is that a return to the senses can serve as a form of resistance or critique. We can trace this idea back further to the early—and often overlooked—writings of Karl Marx. Marx had written of "the sensuous appropriation of the human essence and human life" as key to "the positive supersession of private property."[1] As we have seen, Katchor is himself concerned with labor, production, the commodity form, and the alienation of modern urban life. If his comics turn toward the human senses, they do so because they are implicated in battles over who owns the city and, increasingly, over everyday life itself.

One of the threads running through Katchor's comics is the way in which the human senses are objectified and subjected to market forces. The city is produced as a spectacle to be consumed visually, and corporations seek to profit off of what we see (e.g., "A Look at the Poleax Building," HDA, 45). The sounds we produce can be recorded and sold back to us (e.g., "What Bruno Yule Heard," HDA, 34–35). The print book industry exploits our tactile sense for financial gain no matter the ecological cost (e.g., "The Tragic History of the Oversized Magazine," HDA, 90–91; also in HDA, the untitled endpaper story about Josef Fuss). Of course, books can also have appealing smells. In one story from The Beauty Supply

District, as a business traveler nears an airport newsstand, he is instantly refreshed and exclaims: "Ah, the smell of freshly printed matter!" ("Miniature Snack Kits," *BSD*, 21). In another strip, the idea of consuming media even becomes literal. As the character Emile Delilah places some print materials into his mouth, "The sweet, sharp tang of foreign ink and paper overwhelms his senses" (*CV*, 102).

Katchor understands that exploitative urban work practices dull the human senses. For instance, during Nathan Kishon's tour of the rural commune in *The Jew of New York*, his guide decries these practices and their conditioning of the body: "To pay the rent for an ill-ventilated room above a grog-shop, they are forced to work fifteen hours a day, six days a week. Their one day of rest is spent in a licentious haze of alcohol and frivolous entertainment. They have unwittingly become wage slaves: instruments in the accumulation of capital for a handful of faceless plutocrats" (*JNY*, 29). In such an arrangement, the sensuous pleasures highlighted by Marx—"seeing, hearing, smelling, tasting, feeling, thinking, contemplating, sensing, wanting, acting, loving"[2]—are banished from the working day and relegated to a highly circumscribed zone of weekly activity.

The senses of smell and taste can quite certainly be co-opted into the market economy. Travelers from one of the cultures that Katchor invents in *The Cardboard Valise* always pay with the "scented coins of their realm" (*CV*, 20). Bottle Bay has "cola-flavored waters" (17), and big money is spent in Gazogene City "in an attempt to scientifically determine whether people actually taste the flavor of their favorite beverage" (34). However, other smells given attention by Katchor's narrator, such as those of "ureic acid" (45), "the armpit" (105), and "a freshly sandblasted façade in Old Peek Haboul" (15), are perhaps more likely to resist commodification. Continuing with this theme, the first section of this chapter considers extreme examples of the commodification of scents in a pair of Katchor's most inventive pages, "The Normalcy Parfum Company" (*BSD*, 38) and "Architectural Scents" (*HDA*, 83).

Katchor's interest in smells and tastes goes beyond his critique of the market to address identitarian themes related to the political environment in which he was brought up. The distinction between Yiddish-speaking and Jewish identities that he has made over the years in interviews resonates with debates that unfolded in twentieth-century New York. These debates certainly set the stage for how his father's generation moved through the city's political landscape, and they likely affected the young Katchor as well. Historically speaking,

> The Jewish Socialist movement harbored a range of attitudes toward the twin questions of the nature of Jewish identity and the shape of the Jewish future. Some Socialists, especially among the older comrades who had arrived in America in the 1880s and '90s, struck a resolutely cosmopolitan stance, insisting that they spoke to and for the "Yiddish-speaking," not the "Jewish," proletariat.[3]

Katchor's close examination of culinary matters with close connections to Jewish food culture in *The Dairy Restaurant* does not imply any modification of his firm rejection of dogmatic religion whatsoever. Instead, I would describe his role in this well-researched book as that of the secular scholar.[4] The result of his long-term investigation is an unprecedented textual and visual accounting of the cultural presence and societal impact of New York's Jewish food culture within the broader framework of culinary modernity. The next section of this chapter addresses the smells and tastes associated with New York through discussion of that heavily illustrated book ("Jewish Restaurant Culture in Lower Manhattan," *DR*, 252–53). The chapter closes with a final section on the subject of canned foods by taking on the content and form of a magnificent double-page spread from *Hand-Drying in America* ("Locked Out," *HDA*, 146–47).

Made-to-Order Scents

Smells are ubiquitous in Katchor's fictitious metropolis, and Julius Knipl is a connoisseur. For example, in the first panel of "The Smell of the Post Office" (*JK*, 53), our favorite urban flâneur ventures out at night to check his post office box for mail. Each of the next six panels makes its own contribution to a smorgasbord of inhaled flavors: there is the "smell of rancid finger grease," the "fumes of a day's licked stamps," the "tang of freshly printed junk mail," the "aroma of forty thousand post cards," the "cheap perfume of a hundred thousand commercial love letters," and even the "faint odor of a month's worth of wanted posters under glass." In the last panel, Knipl finds the post office box empty and is denied the "thrilling scent of yet-to-be-delivered mail." Smells are everywhere in Katchor's world, and they run the gamut from the thrilling to the fetid.

Some of the artist's other strips conjecture that even smells, and the emotions we associate with them, come to be grist for the mill of capitalist profiteering. In this not-so-fantastical assertion lies an important history lesson about the market economy itself. First comes a period of relative freedom, during which smells are traded more or less freely, outside the market. One strip from *The Cardboard Valise* tells of a man who invented a way of sending scents over long distances: "By converting the molecular vapors of any object into electromagnetic waves in the radio frequency range, they can be broadcast to a location many miles away where a device I call the 'telodorator' receives, amplifies and converts them back into fumes recognized by the human nose" (*CV*, 27). Next comes the packaging and sale of an individual product, created in small batches. Perhaps it is "the scent of a mimosa tree / Preserved in alcohol and offered for sale in an all-night drug store on Roman Boulevard" ("The Drowned Men's Association," *JK*, 1). Soon after, there comes a large-scale business enterprise.

On the first page of a three-page comic, a salesman for the Normalcy Parfum Company (*BSD*, 37–39) hopes to shift the perfume industry away from its antiquated base in pastoral, rural, and floral scents. Instead of "Hornless Musk Deer," he offers the buyer "Movie Theater Lobby (Popcorn and Air-Conditioned Carpeting)," "Phone Booth, circa 1961," and "Basement Laundromat at 2 a.m." Later, at a sales training seminar, a few "men who answered a classified ad in yesterday's paper" listen to a compelling presentation of the company's innovative vision (fig. 4.1). The key to their success is "simple," achieved merely "by putting a price tag on the residue of everyday life: the smell of a library book, the tang of a brown paper bag, the aroma of door-hinge oil—our new spring line." "Pass them around," the speaker offers encouragingly.

While a close-up shows one future salesman inhaling from the vial of "Pay Phone circa 1961," the textual narrator undercuts the speaker's exuberant performance, noting that "the lecture proceeds late into the night" (panel 5). The panels cut between the neglected decor of a rented room and images of multistory urban exteriors. In the interior scenes, "a few perspiration-stained maps of the city taped to the wall" evoke the desperation of sales that hides behind a slapdash professionalism. The excessive signage on the exterior of the building where they are meeting conveys the saturation of the city by market forces (panels 1 and 8). When the speaker touts the success that Vestal Brothers Department Store has purportedly had in the perfume market, this time it is the visual narrator's turn to undercut the message. The accompanying image shows what is by all appearances a derelict building. Boarding up the front entrance of Vestal Brothers is a warning sign: "Danger. Stay out" (panel 4). It is not the building itself, so much as the industry it represents, that is rotten.

The commodification of daily life, what the Normalcy Parfum Company salesman just referred to as "putting a price tag on the residue of everyday life," recurs as a theme common to many of Katchor's comics. In addition to aforementioned examples like "The After-Rain Business" (*BSD*, 41), "The Crumb Trap" (*HDA*, 54), and "The Lambswoll Hotel" (chap. 1; see fig. 1.4), there is also the example of a character from *The Jew of New York* who anticipates the invention of air-conditioning. "Can you imagine,

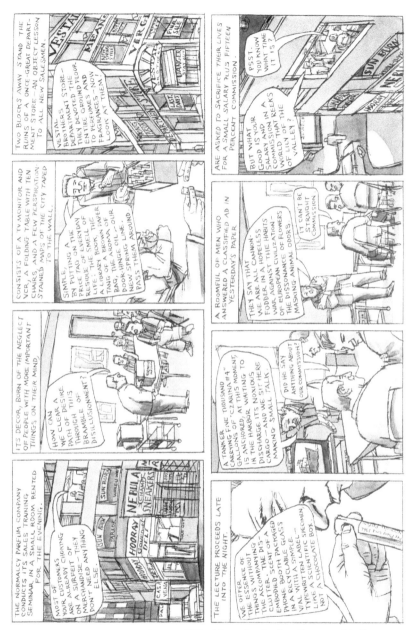

Fig. 4.1. Ben Katchor, second page of "The Normalcy Parfum Company," in *The Beauty Supply District* (Pantheon Books, 2000), 38. Reprinted with the generous permission of Ben Katchor.

making a business out of what falls freely from the sky? What's next, the air we breathe?" (*JNY*, 68). The full-page color strip titled "Architectural Scents" presents an even more ambitious plan to market scents to the modern consumer (fig. 4.2; *HDA*, 83). Instead of making a few calculated tweaks to products in an already successful perfume market, here a "young industrial chemist" creates a portfolio of consumer goods specifically designed to appeal to "aficionados of architecture." These potential customers are "individuals who will go out of their way to visit an unusual building."

The idea illustrated by "Architectural Scents" is to "fabricate a line of personal hygiene products" infused with the scents of noteworthy buildings. The first products in the line feature scents reclaimed from the Tonic House, a nineteenth-century building that was demolished (a reader familiar with Katchor's themes may fairly presume) on account of the redevelopment value of its lot. The chemist makes "a delicate after-bath powder" from the building's crumbled plaster walls, a perfume essence from its yellowed wallpaper, a toothpaste with "a cool, dank flavor" from its stone foundation, and elegant wooden toothpicks from its damaged floorboards. Making money off of old properties is also addressed in the strip "Ornamental Avenue" (*BSD*, 1–3), where one can purchase a photographic postcard series titled "Twenty-Five Views of Ornamental Avenue." (Incidentally, at the time of writing this book, you can buy these postcards on Katchor's website for $16.50.)[5] In "Architectural Scents," however, the idea of selling the past is combined with that of an innovative sales pitch and taken to an extreme. A central panel at the bottom of the page cuts upward across the last two rows of the comic as if the shopping experience it depicts is all-consuming or occupying a greater part of our lives. And, of course, it is. Katchor wants us to know that everything is for sale.

The premise is as absurd as they come: historic preservation meets self-care. Yet, as is usually the case in Katchor's work, under the absurdity lies something quite contemporary. "Architectural Scents" speaks to the way that advances in technology and the

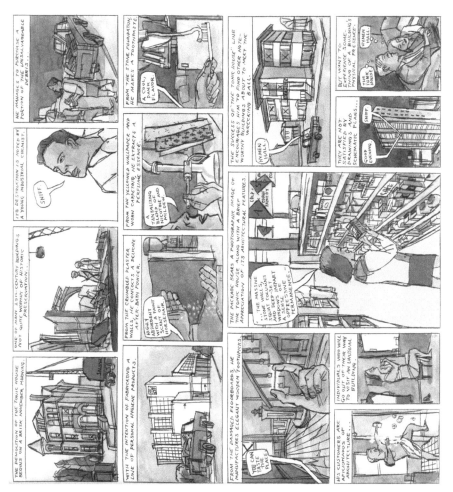

Fig. 4.2. Ben Katchor, "Architectural Scents," in *Hand-Drying in America* (Pantheon Books, 2013), 83. Reprinted with the generous permission of Ben Katchor.

drive toward accumulation have together created highly specific twenty-first-century consumer submarkets. The three panels clustered in the bottom-right corner of the page work together well in this regard. "The success of 'The Tonic House' line encourages [the inventor] to find other noteworthy buildings about to meet the wrecking ball." The strip's final panel implies that the next step lies in developing and distinguishing his-and-hers hygiene lines for architecture aficionados (to the "Tonic House" will be added the "Hymen Hall" line).

The Garden of Eden

Katchor may be quick to poke fun at religion in his strips, but even then, part of the humor still stems from his critique of the market economy—the market's ability to assimilate any topic whatsoever and slap a price tag on it. The two themes may seem to make quite the odd couple. Katchor seems to find joy in fusing them together in new combinations. To the aforementioned example of Tsimtsum Industries ("The Drowned Men's Association," *JK*, 2), one can add Haman's Bar and Grill ("Spontaneous Construction," *HDA*, 8) and the Pharisee Fashion brand ("Fayoum's Finger," *HDA*, 103). Religion is debased as it adheres in spaces of capitalist accumulation, and business's obsession with profit and turnover time is deflated when set against the backdrop of religion's grandiose timescale. The juxtaposition of earthly toil with transcendent belief may itself be an idea of religious origin. Where does one even begin with a brand-name product like "Golden Calf brand pot cheese" (*JK*, 4)? Religion plus advertising: close readers of Katchor's pages will find numerous examples of this hybrid model of humor at work.

The introduction to this book has already called attention to some of the best punch lines from Katchor's comedy set about the Garden of Eden (e.g., "the first recorded instance of a couple splitting a single dish," *DR*, 17). More than twenty-five pages into *The Dairy Restaurant*, he is still at it. For example, take the following mental image created through the use of text and an accompanying two-page drawing, composed in gray tones, of a certain, notable infant sucking on his little finger:

> The angel Gabriel transformed the infant Abraham's right hand into an all-purpose dispenser of food and drink. From his little finger the child could suck milk, from a second finger water, from a third honey, from a fourth the juice of dates, and from his thumb butter. This miracle is today re-created in the common bar-gun or soda-fountain console. (*DR*, 28)

This visual gag is immediately followed by a second punch line: "Only a child suckled on his own hand would have grown into a man filled with the superhuman urge to offer hospitality" (*DR*, 29). Interestingly enough, the "Garden of Eden Restaurant" bit with which *The Dairy Restaurant* begins is anticipated visually in the comic that closes the *Cheap Novelties* re-edition (2016; "The Cheap Merchandise District," *CN*, 108). Exterior and interior scenes of the Garden of Eden Cafeteria occupy the two final pages of the story as Knipl lets himself be talked into a new photography job for *Sexual Prowess Magazine*. In that long-form, volume-concluding comic, sex, food, and religion contribute to an incongruous three-way mash-up from which Katchor extracts no small amount of humor. But make no mistake about it: in *The Dairy Restaurant*, he is quite serious about food.

When Katchor was pushed to describe his forthcoming restaurant history, he asked and answered his own question: "How do you have the pretension to do such a thing? The tone has to be this mock pretension: here it is, from the Garden of Eden to this week, I am going to sum it all up. So it's the tone of an insane person who thinks they can do that."[6] Following dietary law (kashrut), dairy restaurants served fish and vegetables along with milk dishes (milkhiker cuisine), but no meat, as opposed to restaurants that served meat dishes (fleyshiker cuisine), but no dairy.[7] Katchor is most concerned with the twentieth century, but the book has a much wider scope. It moves from biblical times through subjects such as the "seventeenth-century vegetarian renaissance" (*DR*, 76), the eighteenth-century "invention of the restaurant" (124), and dairy-style eating in late-nineteenth-century Warsaw (181), for example.

Katchor once insisted that *The Dairy Restaurant* is "not comics, but a text-image" work, or else a "heavily illustrated" book with "one or two comic-strip moments in it."[8] One of these moments is a reprint of the strip titled "In a Vegetarian Restaurant" that Zuni Maud published in the *Forverts* on August 3, 1919 (*DR*, 304–5). The title and the text of the original are written in Yiddish ("רעסטאָראַנט אין אַ וועגעטאַריאַנישעו").[9] The joke comes in the fifth panel (read right to left in this case), and at the diner's expense. The reason the "vegetarian fish" listed on the menu tastes so good is because the kitchen is in fact preparing real fish. The gag points to large-scale debates. As Katchor's meticulous research bears out, the dairy restaurant in New York intersected with a range of other culinary topics. Beyond the reality that non-Jewish New Yorkers would also have eaten in these restaurants, the dairy restaurant as a culinary phenomenon also intersected with movements of the period that advocated vegetarianism and the health benefits of milk.

The author accomplishes a few interrelated goals over the book's five hundred pages (note that *The Dairy Restaurant* follows in the tradition of *The Cardboard Valise* and *Hand-Drying in America* by putting its paratextual pages to great use). As a matter of course, Katchor delves deeply into the history, evolution, and nuanced exegesis of various culinary matters; he also elucidates the relationship between international influences on dairy restaurants and their larger significance for New York society—not to mention restaurant culture in general. Finally, with pretensions to being exhaustive, he provides a catalog of real New York dairy restaurants with as much information as he can track down: owners, opening and closing dates, menus, matchbooks, dishes, and the like.

While many of the book's illustrations may not warrant classification as comics, readers should exercise caution and not rush to conclusions. For example, take the illustration accompanying a section titled "Jewish Restaurant Culture in Lower Manhattan," which appears in a privileged position, at the book's approximate midpoint (fig. 4.3; *DR*, 252–53). Words in English and Yiddish flood the textual zones of the image, illustrating a point that Katchor himself has made in an interview: "The city is covered with text and so a comic strip that brings image and text together is a strip about the city. There is text in it even if you didn't have these speech balloons and words."[10] In its portrayal of urban density and prominent display of signage, the image reproduces elements of turn-of-the-century newspaper comics. Its main intertextual reference seems to be, most famously, the Yellow Kid, created by Richard F. Outcault in New York.

Certain compositional choices are just as notable. Outcault generally placed the Yellow Kid near the center of his single-panel street scenes, and he used the Kid's sleeping shirt as one more canvas for signage. A slight visual resonance is created by Katchor's decision to place a street urchin in the central foreground. From the letters that can be seen on the pail that he carries, one reads "פּאַרוואַ/parve," whose variants include "פּאַרוועע/parve" and "פּאַרעוו/pareve" in Yiddish, meaning "neutral" and thus not falling into either the meat or the dairy buckets. To the boy's right, stench lines emanate from a fish dropped on the street. In the bottom-left corner is "Magen Bros. Loan Office," written on a parasol. The loan office's name, which is effectively transliterated Hebrew ("מגן/magen," which means "shield"), is yet another touch of light humor.

The Dairy Restaurant dedicates itself to recording a vibrant modern culinary culture in text, and this image is itself a complementary and worthy homage. The drawn street scene pulsates with the vibrancy of the intergenerational and intercultural contributions of waves of eastern European immigrants who, much like Katchor's father, arrived in New York either at the end of the nineteenth century or the beginning of the twentieth. This liveliness endured despite continued pogroms in the Pale of Settlement and the devastation and atrocity of the Shoah, with such restaurants in America

Fig. 4.3. Ben Katchor, "Jewish Restaurant Culture in Lower Manhattan," in *The Dairy Restaurant* (Schocken Books, 2020), 252–53. Reprinted with the generous permission of Ben Katchor.

Jewish Restaurant Culture in Lower Manhattan

We read of Dr. Lilienthal, M. M. Noah, and other luminaries of early American Jewish life of the 1840s and '50s participating in banquets celebrating the Jewish charitable institutions of New York City: the New York Jews' Hospital, the New York Hebrew Assistance Society, etc. These public dinners were held at popular concert- and banquet-hall venues such as the Apollo Saloon, the City Assembly Rooms, or Niblo's Saloon on Broadway, rented for the evening. The banquets, for as many as 600 people, were supplied by caterers, or the kitchen staff of the specific institution sponsoring the event and, according to a contemporary report, were "prepared with great skill and particular regard to our religious rules." The menus ranged from cold meats to "every thing that the season afforded, together with a rich display of all kinds of fruit and choice wines." In honor of Joseph Jacobs, a visiting Jewish lawyer from London in the 1890s, a kosher caterer was engaged to serve a meal at Delmonico's in the style of rarefied pan-European cuisine (Palmettes Varsovienne, Filets de Boeuf aux Olives, etc.).

By the 1860s elaborate Purim costume balls at the 14th Street Academy of Music were an annual fixture among the New York Jewish elite. Nine hundred or so invited guests streamed into the concert hall, which was transformed for the evening into elaborate tableaux vivants from ancient Jewish history. Among the wide range of fanciful costumes could be seen a caricature of a Polish Jew complete with tefillin. The extensive thematic decorations were accompanied by music, "wines and choice edibles." The proceeds went to various Jewish charities.

filling an important social need for transnational Jewish communities. They should be seen as nodes in a food culture that was at once Jewish, Yiddish speaking, and unique to a broad swath of New Yorkers, plain and simple. As the 1980s arrived and the dairy restaurants all but disappeared, the author's conclusion turns to humor to express tragedy. Near the close of *The Dairy Restaurant*, Katchor writes: "I understand that the Jews in those years had experienced a second expulsion from a kind of paradise" (*DR*, 490).[11]

Canned Foods

Even beyond the matter of dairy restaurants and their history, food culture in general carries a heavy load in Katchor's work. Food can be used to demonstrate affection, as in "The Pickled-Tomato Lover" (*JK*, 80), where a woman requires her suitors to steal a jar of her favorite treat if they expect to be invited up to her apartment. Food can entail a sense of risk. In a strip from the *Hotel & Farm* series, "the idea of a canned fruit-cocktail still titillates some people," for whom it provides the same rush as trying to line up lemons, oranges, and cherries on a gambling machine (*H&F*, 175). But some of Katchor's ideas are even more inventive. A strip from *Cheap Novelties* has the Health Department investing in "a number of public mustard fountains in the midtown area," to the presumed delight of the lunch crowd (*CN*, 85). In "The Surgical Supply Shop" (*JK*, 66), a salesman touts the latest in medical innovations, which now include "boiled cabbage serum injections" and "brisket of beef grafts." These examples may be far-fetched, but they seem strangely familiar all the same. Food is polysemic in Katchor's comics because it is polysemic in our own world.

Katchor holds restaurants and cafés in high esteem for more than just their food. They are places where something special or unexpected can often happen. There was the example of Yosl Feinbroyt's transcendent café vision in *The Jew of New York* (chap. 2; see figs. 2.3, 2.4). And it is no surprise that a cafeteria serves as the setting for the culminating scene of Knipl's "The Cheap Merchandise District" (*CN*, 108–9). In another strip, what Knipl hears in the Sigmoid Restaurant sends him down memory lane ("The Overheard Order," *JK*, 65). Katchor's comics can also serve up more routine fare. At the Rialto Delicatessen, customers lose their appetite once they see a wall of celebrity photographs (*CN*, 83). Restaurant owners sometimes have to accept "the inevitable disappearance of salt and pepper shakers, oil and vinegar bottles, knives, forks and spoons" as the cost of doing business (*CN*, 70). I like to think that "Hoodornament" (*BSD*, 40) depicts Katchor himself, disguised as a character who sits "all day in this coffee shop scribbling on paper napkins, drinking strong tea and contemplating the lunch menu."

Canned foods seem to be particularly charged with metaphorical power. In "The Overheard Order," somewhat magically, "the milk of human kindness, condensed into a dented sixteen-ounce can, turns up on a shelf outside the men's room" (*JK*, 65). That there may be an aura surrounding canned food is to be expected when discussing a generation perhaps influenced by Warhol. But there is nothing "pop" about Katchor's richly detailed close-ups of cans of "Protose Vegetable Meat" (*DR*, 291) or "Orphanage Brand Tender Seedless Grapes" ("Canned-Food Tastings," *JK*, 52). The depth of these images—the artist's use of light, shadow, shading, and perspective—pushes us beyond the surface toward a corresponding depth of thinking.

In "Canned-Food Tastings," Katchor dramatizes an entire urban scene of backroom, invitation-only tastings where canned foods are savored and categorized by date, label, and embossed lot number (*JK*, 52). Elsewhere he develops an elaborate canned-food mythology. In *The Cardboard Valise*, the narrator says that "the very act of can opening is laden with ritual significance." Canned food is elevated to a culinary delicacy. The last panel of this latter strip informs us that "in the Pantheon of canned foods, pea soup, of all things, has been given a place of honor and mystical distinction" (*CV*, 18). In another strip, a man visiting Tensint

Island tells his taxi driver that "I want a taste of that real island cuisine—something straight from the can." Riding in the back seat, he thinks, "At these tourist restaurants everything is done with an electric can-opener; the cans sit around open for hours before you're served. I know a little place on the south coast where they use only hand-openers of the gouge and push variety. The food goes from the dark of the can to the dark of your stomach" (*CV*, 20).

One can only speculate why canned foods have this allure for Ben Katchor. They can certainly serve the same variety of artistic needs as other foods—in terms of both narrative and humor, that is. Perhaps in an even more obvious way than agricultural and unprocessed foods, canned foods bring into relief the larger system of food production, packaging, and delivery. They are manufactured goods. The can is clearly the end result of a production chain. There is something deceptive about the way the can hides business, profit, and all the labor that went into its creation. All these associations overlap with the artist's preferred themes.

Having just discussed *The Dairy Restaurant*, it also seems relevant to note that

> between 1914 and 1924, consumption of kosher meat in New York City fell by 25 to 30 percent. At the same time, many Jews transferred their previous concern for ritual purity to an interest in high sanitary standards in processed foods. . . . By the 1920s, many Jews had abandoned *kashrut* altogether, embracing instead a modern preference for recognizable brands of packaged goods with reliably predictable quality.[12]

If we keep such a historical context in mind, then canned foods are many things in Katchor's work. They reflect the reality of what any mid-twentieth-century New Yorker would consume. They are a point of entry into discussing manufacturing chains. Above all else, they seem to encapsulate an idea the artist has put into words quite well himself in one of his strips: canned foods connote "the romance of industrial production" ("Industrial Luxuries,"

HDA, 155). As such they serve as a visual metaphor for certain ideas surrounding loneliness, joy, human connection, and even modern design.

No strip speaks to Katchor's interest in the metaphorical connotations of canned foods more than "Locked Out" (HDA, 146–47). The form of the two-page comic is itself worthy of note (figs. 4.4, 4.5). A series of yellow-washed panels form a ring around two larger central panels in blue. The location and function of these blue panels illustrate a design decision that Katchor has explained in interviews: "There's a kind of panel in some of the strips that sits outside the rest of the time frame." In these situations, such a panel "leaves the grid," and thus the page's reading path is "not just a linear thing."[13] As Katchor explains, "So it's like, the design of the page of the Talmud where you have a main text and then you have commentaries on texts."[14]

The yellow and the blue panels of this comic can be considered relatively autonomous documents. The main text of the blue panels turns the opening of a can of sardines into a visual metaphor. "If the sardine can embodied the dilemmas of modern life . . . / the key served as a mechanism for alleviating our anxiety." Through qualities such as the size of the panels, the close-ups of the sardine tins, and the before-and-after sequencing of the two images, readers are encouraged to see this main text as a bite-size instruction for living. The lack of surrounding detail in the second blue panel and the visual repetition of a can being opened convey the solemnity of a parable. In the verso blue panel, the content of a word balloon offers an even more allegorical or metatextual statement: "organic forms squeezed into a geometric container." The formal structure of the panels encourages readers to see this as a metaphor for the human condition. Particularly in a dense city like New York, urban living is, in many respects, this very thing: humans squeezed into geometric containers. One thinks of the "Enthrall News" vendor and the magazine reader of "On the Newsstand" (chap. 3; see fig. 3.2), each enclosed within his respective container—either a kiosk or an apartment building. The thought is simultaneously

Fig. 4.4. Ben Katchor, first page of "Locked Out," in *Hand-Drying in America* (Pantheon Books, 2013), 146. Reprinted with the generous permission of Ben Katchor.

Fig. 4.5. Ben Katchor, second page of "Locked Out," in *Hand-Drying in America* (Pantheon Books, 2013), 147. Reprinted with the generous permission of Ben Katchor.

a reflection on the comics medium. To create comics, one has to squeeze lives into small geometric containers—using techniques of visual, iconic representation, of course.

Marked historical elements appear in the commentary text provided in the yellow-washed panels. Katchor applies the lens of the class character of modern life in his exegesis of the sardine key's social role. Class distinctions were minimized as the key "offered unlimited access to all levels of society." Technologically speaking, the key was "a marked improvement over the levered punch opener." In the far-right middle panel, this punch opener hovers over a background image, much as the Julius Knipl–stamped objects did throughout the *Cheap Novelties* strips (figs. 1.1, 3.1). The bottom-left corner panel contains a similarly floating image of an easy-open sardine can for which a key is no longer necessary. While the advent of the sardine key placed us in a productive and emotionally fulfilling relationship with our canned food, Katchor's narrator sees the shift toward easy-open tabs in negative terms.

Taste is both literal and figurative in the strip. In the final panel, the protagonist loses his taste for sardines, but this is connected with a downturn in social taste. Larger forces are in play. The narrator points out that "a coarseness pervaded all areas of industrial production. / A heavy hand was evident in architectural design. / Brute force was applied to everything." As the man stares out of the square windowpanes of the geometric container that is his apartment, there is a palpable feeling of obsolescence, one made perhaps more playfully in "Euro Trash / American Garbage" (chap. 2). The point made by "Locked Out" is that it is the human consumer who is obsolete. The sardine key placed him in an active relationship to his food ("The turning of the wrist coupled with a sense of trepidation imparted a special flavor to the fish"). But now the consumer is one more passive object. We are all "victims of design," unable to participate in the construction of the modern city.[15] We are expendable, mere inhabitants and consumers rather than makers, passive vehicles for profit and capital accumulation.

Conclusion

In a midlength book such as this, quite a bit gets left out, and the author has no choice but to grapple with feelings of regret. So as to not wallow in feelings of incompletion, I will keep this brief.

Some of my favorite strips of all time didn't make it into this book at all. "The Stair Cake" (*HDA*, 55) seems more relevant than ever with the 2022 debut of a Netflix television show called *Is It Cake?* The way Katchor's fascinations with fluids and urban systems come together in the humorous depiction of a citywide scandal in "Liquid Soap Theft" (*JK*, 36) reflects the artist at his best. The suggestion that a dinner-plate garnish like parsley could make its own contribution to the atmosphere of the "Horish House Hotel" dining room was a true gem (*H&F*, 181). I laughed so many times reading "The Deep Tub" (*HDA*, 68) that I thought about purchasing an archival inkjet print from Ben's website. (I ended up doing so just as this book went to press.)

Although this book's concise chapters touch on a wide range of interconnected themes, various ways of seeing Katchor's comics remain underexplored or even absent. The more I considered his oeuvre, the more it resonated with me as a scholar of urban cultural studies. Finishing this book has convinced me that his text and image work truly deserves a more careful and sustained analysis from that perspective, one that explicitly addresses insights from a century of urban theory. My intention to make this book as accessible as possible, for that contrivance known as "the general reader," kept me from going on and on about Henri Lefebvre's *Critique of Everyday Life*, and his fundamental questioning regarding who has "the right to the city." By instead including many references to biographical questions and Katchor's own statements in interviews, I have stayed close to the central premise of the Biographix series.

I purposely chose not to delve too far into the notion of Jewish comics or the artist's debatable classification in reference to competing understandings of that label. (See, for example, the book *Visualizing Jewish Narrative: Jewish Comics and Graphic Novels*, edited by Derek Parker Royal, where panels by Katchor are used as the cover art.) Although I have written here and there of Yiddish-speaking and eastern European New York identities in this book, Katchor's own comments on authors like Sholem Aleichem, I. L. Peretz, and especially Isaac Bashevis Singer have opened my eyes to possible themes for future research. More might be written, too, about Katchor's interest in mysticism, and especially Kabbalah, as it intersects with the market economy in the history of the United States. (One last recommendation: Brian Ogren's book *Kabbalah and the Founding of America*.)

Some of the richest possibilities for future research by comics scholars are to be found in what Thierry Groensteen called the recitation (textual narration) and monstration (visual narration) of Katchor's works. Not only do his comics engage in prolepsis and analepsis in splendid ways, but his text in particular—for me at least—recalls the blurred discourse, and the grand style, of prose literature from the apogee of the nineteenth-century novel, continuing through the mid-twentieth century. There are fusions of voices, an indeterminate hovering between first- and third-person narration, a refusal to settle into a limited perspective. An omniscience, but with preoccupations of its own, stepping into the subjectivity of character. Free indirect style, one might call it.

I ask readers for forgiveness. Undoubtedly, there are appearances of Ben Katchor's work that I have missed for one reason or another. As compensation I can offer only my hope that I have included an early comic or two that fans might have missed. "Italian Ices" (1988) seemed to be most deserving of extended treatment, and "The Corner Location" (1989) is a splendid nod to the architectural form of comics (see introduction). I would heartily recommend a number of web comics available on his website in the "Our Mental Age" tab (http://katchor.com/Our_Mental_Age. html). I understand that Katchor is currently preparing a book of his strips from the *Shoehorn Technique* series, which ran in the English-language *Forward* and a few other weeklies from 2004 to 2006. A collection of the *Hotel & Farm* series should also be forthcoming.

Still, one cannot help but think that maybe all these feelings of incompletion and regret are a fitting response to Ben Katchor's comics world and its depiction of a transitory urban world.

NOTES

1. It is often remarked that Katchor was the first cartoonist to be named a MacArthur fellow. However, Charles Johnson received the fellowship in 1998. Admittedly, the work that Johnson (1948–) produced trended toward prose in the decades before receiving the recognition. But he made cartoons in high school, and then for his college and local newspapers, before drawing hundreds of cartoons from 1968 to 1973 and publishing the books *Black Humor* (1970) and *Half-Past Nation Time* (1972). See Johnson's essay and profile published in *It's Life as I See It: Black Cartoonists in Chicago, 1940–1980* (2021), edited by Dan Nadel.

2. Katchor, in Royal 2018 [2015], 160, also 169.

3. Katchor, in Balcaen 2018 [2014], 139–40.

4. Balcaen 2018 [2014], 139–40.

5. Regarding the origin of *The Jew of New York*, Katchor reports that he proposed something with a Jewish-sounding title after the editors told him that the weekly strips he was doing at the time were not Jewish enough (email correspondence with the artist).

6. Katchor, in Aldama 2017.

7. Katchor, in Korver 2018 [2008], 60.

8. Katchor, in Santoro 2018 [1996], 12.

9. I would include in this list Charles Baudelaire, Walter Benjamin, Jane Jacobs, Henri Lefebvre, Lewis Mumford, Georg Simmel, and Louis Wirth, among many others.

10. See Simmel 2010 [1903].

11. See Jacobs 1992 [1961].

12. Katchor, in Theroux 2018 [2004], 53.

13. Katchor, in Balcaen 2018 [2014], 138. Also, "Actually only my father was a communist fellow-traveler. Yiddish was his first language; my mother's second" (Katchor, added in 2017 to Birnbaum 2018 [2000], 33). See also another comment on his father: "He was born in Warsaw. It was that wave of Eastern European immigration. He came in the twenties or thirties, via Brazil, so he was a late arrival chronologically" (Katchor, in Adams 2018 [2011], 70).

14. Katchor, in Theroux 2018 [2004], 55; Katchor, in Adams 2018 [2011], 74.

15. Katchor, in Adams 2018 [2011], 74. See also: "So, although I have these familial connections to old-world traditional Jewish culture of a particular sort (nineteenth- and early twentieth-century Warsaw), those connections are very tenuous and not a tradition I'm consciously trying to uphold. So, national or ethnic identity (like patriotism) is for people who are afraid of being judged for what they are making of their own life and want to ride, in a mob, on the coattails of their supposedly venerable ancestors. Racial identity is just a dangerous fantasy. The word 'Jewish' without a long string of qualifiers and explanations is a totally nebulous term, except to an ignorant anti-semite who thinks he knows exactly what it means" (Katchor, in Royal 2018 [2015], 157–58).

16. Katchor, in Korver 2018 [2008], 61.

17. "Yiddish was one of the two languages I was exposed to as a child. As it was my father's first language, endearments, jokes, and qualitative descriptions were all expressed in that language. I was also aware that it was a language connected to a secular Jewish culture whose development was truncated, in part, by WWII. Each year, my father took me to a public commemoration of the Warsaw ghetto uprising and destruction. This event was conducted in Yiddish. My interest in Yiddish culture was through recorded music and writing in Yiddish and so the sound of that language evokes a parallel culture of humor and politics. I resisted my father's attempts to teach me to read Yiddish as a child, but in my twenties learned to read it. The effect of Yiddish on my own work is that of seeing English through the lens of a language with different ways of describing the world" (Katchor, in Balcaen 2018 [2014], 143–44).

18. "We lived in Bed-Stuy and most of his [my father's] friends were Yiddish speakers. There were always Yiddish papers, like the *Freiheit* in the house. He took me to all these Yiddish cultural events, concerts, lectures, plays, all before the first grade. Those years were a whole life, an eternity. That's a long time for a little kid, all these incredible events. He would drag me along on errands to the Lower East Side; I used to like to go along. He wanted me to be able to function in Yiddish, but not so much that he forced me to study it. I didn't really use it, I always spoke English" (Katchor, in Portnoy 2018 [2013], 136).

19. "I did one strip in Yiddish: 'A Frage fun Koni Ilend.' I did it in 1983 but it was never published but I posted it online years later" (Katchor, added in 2017 to Santoro 2018 [1996], 9). See also his comments in Royal 2018 [2015], 157.

20. Katchor, in Birnbaum 2018 [2012], 98.

21. Katchor, in Portnoy 2018 [2013], 135; *DR*, 66, 92, 153, 428, 440.

22. Katchor, in Birnbaum 2018 [2012], 90; see also related comments in Adams 2018 [2011], 70.

23. "That Eastern European culture was intact when I was a kid and abruptly died off, maybe in the mid-sixties. It's hard to say when it died. There are people still who

were kids then, a little older than me, who are still a part of that culture and are still around" (Katchor, in Adams 2018 [2011], 70).

24. This general idea and the foregoing quotation are borrowed from Ian Hague's landmark text *Comics and the Senses* (2014, 3).

25. I use this word "signifies" in the sense that Thierry Groensteen gives it in *Comics and Narration* (2013).

26. See Davies 2019; Fraser 2019; Dittmer 2014; Ahrens and Meteling 2010.

27. Certain comics authors take the architecture of page design to an extreme. For instance, Chris Ware is known for layering small panels as if they were bricks, or using cutaway images of a house so that its very rooms provide the comic's panel structure. See chapter 1 of Mélanie Van de Hoorn's *Bricks and Balloons* (2012). This cutaway design was, of course, also used by numerous others before Ware, including by Will Eisner in his iconic strip *The Spirit*.

28. Here I refer to what Andrei Molotiu (2012) calls the iconostatic quality of comics.

29. For similarly innovative projects that play with the materiality of the book format, see the French-language work of Marc-Antoine Matthieu.

CHAPTER 1. SIGHT

1. Feldman 2009, 130; Gardner 2006, 790–91; Murphy 2002, 159.

2. Murphy 2002, 159; on the word "knipl," Murphy 2002, 159–60; see also Weschler 1993, and discussion in Fraser 2019, 130–35.

3. Katchor, in McWeeney 2018 [2000], 26.

4. Feldman 2009, 130.

5. Op de Beeck 2006, 817.

6. Katchor 2002, 4.

7. Katchor stated that "my father . . . was an atheist, a utopian socialist who subscribed to the *Freiheit*, the Yiddish-language Communist daily paper" (Katchor, in Portnoy 2018 [2013], 136).

8. Polland and Soyer 2012, 187, also 173–74, 186.

9. Moore 2004, 480.

10. Gregory-Guider 2005, para. 10.

11. See Katchor's comments in Balcaen 2018 [2014], 150: "Our relations with people are mediated by objects and sometimes the object can replace the person in our interest."

12. For example, "The explorer Rudolf Maennerchor travels to Tensint Island determined to find living proof of an authentic native culture. . . . This can't be all there is: restroom ruins and canned food—the scourings of western civilization!" (*CV*, 23).

13. Katchor has said that "these objects were meant to be an endless series of promotional giveaways ordered to be manufactured, or hoped to be, by Knipl to help promote his business. As I recall, only one, a ballpoint pen imprinted with his name

and address, appears in the longer story. An actual "Knipl" ballpoint pen giveaway was produced to promote the publication of *Cheap Novelties*" (email correspondence with artist).

14. Miriam Katin, in Baskind 2010, 242.

15. Pascal Lefèvre (2009) calls this space the *hors cadre*.

16. By visual narration I refer to the concept of a distinction between written narration (recitation) and visual narration (monstration); see Groensteen 2013; Mikkonen 2017. My intention is to keep such analytical terms out of the body text of this book as a way of reaching the general reader.

17. Katchor, in Cometbus 2018 [2016], 181.

18. These spaces are what Pascal Lefèvre (2009) calls the *hors champs*.

19. This section's analysis draws from the spatial theory and urban thinking of Henri Lefebvre, specifically his book *The Survival of Capitalism* (1976), and his three-volume *Critique of Everyday Life* (1947, 1961, 1981). See also Fraser, *Toward an Urban Cultural Studies* (2015).

20. From Katchor, in Balcaen 2018 [2014], 138; see also Katchor, in Gordon 2018 [2017], 213.

21. Op de Beeck 2006, 817.

CHAPTER 2. HEARING

1. I am thinking of *Musicophilia*, by Oliver Sacks (2007), and *This Is Your Brain on Music*, by Daniel Levitin (2006).

2. See also Katchor's comments in McWeeney 2018 [2000], 27–28.

3. Katchor has also worked with "Bang on a Can (Michael Gordon, David Lang, and Julia Wolfe), Moritz Eggert, [and] Bob McGrath (Ridge Theater)." Katchor, in Balcaen 2018 [2014], 149. See information on *The Carbon Copy Building* and *There Was a Building, or The 58th Street Broiler* at https://katchor.com/other-collaborations.html.

4. Drawing on Frank L. Cioffi's discussion of the spoken qualities of Katchor's narration, Ian Hague has made the case that the Julius Knipl audio pieces should be accepted as comics (Hague 2014, 82–84). Hague also asserts that what he calls "the drawn strip without a drawn strip" (84) is a perfect illustration of Katchor's interests in themes of loss, absence, erosion, and time.

5. Katchor, in Theroux 2018 [2004], 54. "My strips begin with a written script. It's easier for me to write than draw—it's less of an investment of time and I can do it lying on my back. Once I begin drawing, the text is altered to function alongside the image. I see what can be better expressed with a concrete image. The abstract words take their proper place in the spectrum of the meaning."

6. That is, in the beginning, God contracted to make room for creation. See Gershom Scholem, *Major Trends in Jewish Mysticism* (1995 [1941]), 260. "According to Luria, God was compelled to make room for the world by, as it were, abandoning a

region within Himself, a kind of mystical primordial space from which He withdrew in order to return to it in the act of creation and revelation" (261).

7. References are to the Ladino (Judeo-Spanish) and Yiddish (Judeo-German) languages.

8. Scholem 1995 [1941], 120, 123, 129.

9. In the thirteenth century, during Abraham Abulafia's time, there was a surge of interest in Kabbalah in Spain and southern France, which later blossomed in sixteenth-century Sefad and came to influence Orthodox Judaism and Haredi communities more generally, as well as certain conservative and reform traditions.

10. The next page refers to the episode as "an ascent through the seventh palace of the seventh heaven" (*JNY*, 34). On Merkabah/throne mysticism, the seven heavens, and the book of Ezekiel, see Scholem 2015 [1960].

11. A later segment of *The Jew of New York* featuring Feinbroyt continues with this theme. He approaches the publisher of a new American dictionary and informs him of his great progress: "I have a catalog of six hundred echoic words derived from the processes of eating and digestion—a completely ignored realm of human discourse. These orphaned words must be given their rightful place in the American language" (*JNY*, 78). The publisher is not interested, and the last panel of the strip has Feinbroyt out on the street, reading his entry for the word *grepts* aloud to passersby. This too recalls Abulafia's own lack of popularity.

CHAPTER 3. TOUCH

1. Hague 2014, 98; on virtual media and tactility, see the discussion on p. 96, where he draws on the work of Laura U. Marks.

2. See Baetans and Lefèvre 2014 [1993].

3. Katchor, in Balcaen 2018 [2014], 150; in Theroux 2018 [2004], 58.

4. See Aldama 2017.

5. Gordon 2018 [2017], 215.

6. Katchor, in Royal and Kunka 2018 [2013], 113; see also Katchor's reflections on the economics of the publishing industry, 123.

7. Katchor, in Cometbus 2018 [2016], 179; see also Gravett 2001, 26. In *The Dairy Restaurant*, Katchor provides the year along with more information: "In 1995, having lost the print venue for my weekly comic strip, *Julius Knipl, Real Estate Photographer*, I constructed an 187 x 24-inch illuminated Plexiglas box to display the ongoing episodes of the strip in public and somehow convinced Beatrice Poznanski, then owner of the B&H, to allow me to place that box in the window of her restaurant" (*DR*, 484).

8. Katchor, in Birnbaum 2018 [2012], 91; and Katchor 2002, 4.

9. The full-page comics story taken up in the book's front and back matter arguably continues on (unnumbered) pages 105 and 120 of *The Cardboard Valise*.

10. Intriguingly, an earlier comic from *Cheap Novelties* shows a similar close-up of a hand holding a playing card, as if the reader is inhabiting the same space as the character in the story (*CN*, 49).

11. The allegory through which the life cycle of books is used to reflect on the human condition becomes concrete in the last empaneled comic of the collection. While the suitcase at the beginning of the collection was filled with unwanted books as a way of testing the weight limits of a flimsy cardboard, the suitcase in the comic at the end of the volume holds the living body of one Boreal Rince. Rince is a native of Fluxion City who manages to smuggle himself on an airplane to Outer Canthus. Katchor thus substitutes the old medical textbooks for a human body. The transience and liminal status implied in travel become a metaphor for this brief earthly life.

12. Katchor, in Royal and Kunka 2018 [2013], 116.

13. See similar comments made by Katchor in Royal 2018 [2015], 162: "Ecologically print is a disaster; culturally it was available only to people with the capital to underwrite it."

14. Katchor, in Birnbaum 2018 [2012], 85. In *The Jew of New York*, Katchor also discusses the excesses of print, with these words spoken by a character: "There are high speed steam presses in Boston and New York spewing out more printed material than can ever be consumed—over three hundred thousand bibles and six million tracts last year alone" (*JNY*, 23).

CHAPTER 4. SMELL/TASTE

1. On Marx and the human senses, see the discussion in Fraser, *Visible Cities* (2019, chap. 2, 52–54), as well as Marx, *Economic and Philosophical Manuscripts of 1844*, particularly the essay "Private Property and Communism" (Marx 1977).

2. See Marx 1977, 91; and the discussion in Merrifield 2002, 78.

3. Polland and Soyer 2012, 160–61.

4. As he has said, "A rabbi is just a scholar" (in Adams 2018 [2011], 73); quite a few years before the book was finally published, he noted that "I'm researching dairy restaurants and wanted to get an idea of the contemporary Orthodox view of these matters" (in Theroux 2018 [2004], 56).

5. See https://katchor.com/books-prints-postcards.html.

6. Katchor, in Roth 2018 [2016], 203.

7. Katchor, in Cometbus 2018 [2016], 179. "They were restaurants that followed a Jewish dietary law, where you couldn't mix milk and meat dishes together. Grains, vegetables, even fish was okay, but not meat. It was an arcane law that influenced a whole part of restaurant culture. I go into that in the book—the place of this in the bigger world." See also Polland and Soyer 2012, 133.

8. See Katchor, in Roth 2018 [2016], 202–3.

9. In a dissertation titled "The Creation of a Jewish Cartoon Space in the New York and Warsaw Yiddish Press 1884–1939," Edward Portnoy coins the term "visual midrash" to refer to "one of the most interesting and salient features of Yiddish cartoons," namely, "their heavy reliance on traditional Jewish themes for use as metaphors commenting on current issues" (Portnoy 2008, 212).

10. Katchor, in McWeeney 2018 [2000], 29. The quotation continues: "The narration of the city is such that it is part of this city, this urban world. It's insane outside with the density of signage in Times Square." Katchor's comic "Logo Rage" (*HDA*, 158) deals with the psychological effects of being repeatedly exposed to a certain branded word-image combination.

11. The whole quote reads as follows: "Through the 1970s, the dairy restaurant had seemed to be an eternal presence in the restaurant culture of New York. The remarkable fragility of their existence—dependent upon the rare confluence of ancient Jewish dietary law and the eighteenth-century invention of the restaurant—was completely taken for granted. Now that they are almost completely gone, I understand that the Jews in those years had experienced a second expulsion from a kind of paradise" (*DR*, 490).

12. Polland and Soyer 2012, 128–29.

13. Katchor, in Royal and Kunka, *Comics Alternative Podcast*, March 13, 2013, mins. 27–28.

14. Katchor, in Royal and Kunka 2018 [2013], 117.

15. Katchor, in Royal and Kunka 2018 [2013], 120–21.

BIBLIOGRAPHY

WORKS BY BEN KATCHOR

Katchor, Ben. 2016 [1991]. *Cheap Novelties: The Pleasures of Urban Decay*. Montreal: Drawn & Quarterly.

Katchor, Ben. 2013. *Hand-Drying in America and Other Stories*. New York: Pantheon Books.

Katchor, Ben. 2011. *The Cardboard Valise*. New York: Pantheon Books.

Katchor, Ben. 2004. "Hotel & Farm." *McSweeney's Quarterly Concern*, no. 13. Edited by Chris Ware. New York: Penguin Books.

Katchor, Ben. 2002. "Hotel & Farm." *Art Journal* 61 (3): 4–5, 28–31, 40–45, 74–77, 88–91.

Katchor, Ben. 2000. *Julius Knipl, Real Estate Photographer: The Beauty Supply District*. New York: Pantheon Books.

Katchor, Ben. 1998. *The Jew of New York*. New York: Pantheon Books.

Katchor, Ben. 1996. *Julius Knipl, Real Estate Photographer: Stories*. New York: Little, Brown.

Katchor, Ben. 1990 [1989]. "The Corner Location." *Raw* 2 (2): 180–82.

Katchor, Ben. 1988. "Italian Ices." *Bad News* 3:3–6.

INTERVIEWS WITH BEN KATCHOR

Adams, Sam. 2018 [2011]. "Interview." Originally published in *A.V. Club*. Reprinted in *Ben Katchor: Conversations*, edited by Ian Gordon, 63–76. Jackson: University Press of Mississippi.

Aldama, Frederick Luis. 2017. "An Unexpected Life through Comics: An Interview with Ben Katchor." *Studies in 20th and 21st Century Literature* 42 (1): article 11. https://doi.org/10.4148/2334-4415.1975.

Balcaen, Alexandre. 2018 [2014]. "Interview." Originally published in the French comics magazine *DMPP*. Reprinted in *Ben Katchor: Conversations*, edited by Ian Gordon, 138–51. Jackson: University Press of Mississippi.

Birnbaum, Robert. 2018 [2000]. "Ben Katchor." Originally published in *Identity Theory*. Reprinted in *Ben Katchor: Conversations*, edited by Ian Gordon, 33–40. Jackson: University Press of Mississippi.

Cometbus, Aaron. 2018 [2016]. "Interview with Ben Katchor." Originally published in *Cometbus*, no. 57. Reprinted in *Ben Katchor: Conversations*, edited by Ian Gordon, 179–85. Jackson: University Press of Mississippi.

Gordon, Ian. 2018 [2017]. "Katchor Interview." In *Ben Katchor: Conversations*, edited by Ian Gordon, 207–16. Jackson: University Press of Mississippi.

Korver, Steve. 2018 [2008]. "Being a New Yorker in New York." Originally published in *Amsterdam Weekly*. Reprinted in *Ben Katchor: Conversations*, edited by Ian Gordon, 60–62. Jackson: University Press of Mississippi.

McWeeney, Catherine. 2018 [2000]. "A Conversation with Ben Katchor." Originally published in *Bold Type* 4 (4). Reprinted in *Ben Katchor: Conversations*, edited by Ian Gordon, 26–32. Jackson: University Press of Mississippi.

Portnoy, Eddie. 2018 [2013]. "The Prosen People." Originally published in *Jewish Book Council Blog*. Reprinted in *Ben Katchor: Conversations*, edited by Ian Gordon, 135–37. Jackson: University Press of Mississippi.

Roth, Gil. 2018 [2016]. "An Interview with Ben Katchor." Originally published in *Virtual Memories Show*, no. 191. Reprinted in *Ben Katchor: Conversations*, edited by Ian Gordon, 193–206. Jackson: University Press of Mississippi.

Royal, Derek Parker. 2018 [2015]. "Picturing American Stories: An Interview with Ben Katchor." Originally published in *Unfinalized Moments*. Reprinted in *Ben Katchor: Conversations*, edited by Ian Gordon, 155–78. Jackson: University Press of Mississippi. 155–78.

Royal, Derek Parker, and Andrew J. Kunka. 2018 [2013]. "The Comics Alternative Interview with Ben Katchor." Originally published in *Comics Alternative Podcast*, no. 28. Reprinted in *Ben Katchor: Conversations*, edited by Ian Gordon, 111–26. Jackson: University Press of Mississippi.

Royal, Derek Parker, and Andrew J. Kunka. 2013. Interview with Ben Katchor, March 13, 2013. *Comics Alternative Podcast*.

Santoro, Frank. 2018 [1996]. "An Interview with Ben Katchor." Originally published in *Destroy All Comics*, no. 5. Reprinted in *Ben Katchor: Conversations*, edited by Ian Gordon, 3–19. Jackson: University Press of Mississippi.

Theroux, Alexander. 2018 [2004]. "Ben Katchor." Originally published in *Bomb* 88. Reprinted in *Ben Katchor: Conversations*, edited by Ian Gordon, 50–59. Jackson: University Press of Mississippi.

OTHER REFERENCES

Ahrens, Jörn, and Arno Meteling, eds. 2010. *Comics and the City: Urban Space in Print, Picture and Sequences*. New York: Continuum.

Baetans, Jan, and Pascal Lefèvre. 2014 [1993]."The Work and Its Surround." In *The French Comics Theory Reader*, edited by Ann Miller and Bart Beaty, 191–202. Leuven: Leuven University Press.

Baskind, Samantha. 2010. "A Conversation with Miriam Katin." In *The Jewish Graphic Novel: Critical Approaches*, edited by Samantha Baskind and Ranen Omer-Sherman, 237–43. New Brunswick, NJ: Rutgers University Press.

Cioffi, Frank L. 2001. "Disturbing Comics: The Disjunction of Word and Image in the Comics of Andrzej Mleczko, Ben Katchor, R. Crumb, and Art Spiegelman." In *The Language of Comics: Word and Image*, edited by Robin Varnum and Christina T. Gibbons, 97–122. Jackson: University Press of Mississippi.

Davies, Dominic. 2019. *Urban Comics: Infrastructure and the Global City in Contemporary Graphic Narratives*. London: Routledge.

Dittmer, Jason, ed. 2014. *Comic Book Geographies*. Stuttgart: Franz Steiner.

Feldman, Mark. 2009. "The Urban Studies of Ben Katchor." In *Teaching the Graphic Novel*, edited by Stephen E. Tabachnick, 129–36. New York: MLA.

Fraser, Benjamin. 2019. *Visible Cities, Global Comics: Urban Images and Spatial Form*. Jackson: University Press of Mississippi.

Fraser, Benjamin. 2015. *Toward an Urban Cultural Studies: Henri Lefebvre and the Humanities*. New York: Palgrave Macmillan.

Gardner, Jared. 2006. "Archives, Collectors, and the New Media Work of Comics." *Modern Fiction Studies* 52 (4): 787–806.

Gravett, Paul. 2001. "After Maus." *Jewish Quarterly* 48 (4): 21–28.

Gregory-Guider, Christopher C. 2005. "Sinclair's *Rodinsky's Room* and the Art of Autobiography." *Literary London: Interdisciplinary Studies in the Representation of London* 3 (2): n.p.

Groensteen, Thierry. *Comics and Narration*. Translated by Ann Miller. Jackson: University Press of Mississippi.

Hague, Ian. 2014. *Comics and the Senses: A Multisensory Approach to Comics and Graphic Novels*. New York: Routledge.

Jacobs, Jane. 1992 [1961]. *The Life and Death of Great American Cities*. New York: Vintage.

Lefebvre, Henri. 2005 [1986]. *Critique of Everyday Life*. Vol. 3. Translated by Gregory Elliott. New York: Verso.

Lefebvre, Henri. 2002 [1961]. *Critique of Everyday Life*. Vol. 2. Translated by John Moore. New York: Verso.

Lefebvre, Henri. 1991 [1947]. *Critique of Everyday Life*. Vol. 1. Translated by John Moore. New York: Verso.

Lefebvre, Henri. 1976. *The Survival of Capitalism: Reproduction of the Relations of Production*. Translated by Frank Bryant. New York: St. Martin's Press.

Lefèvre, Pascal. 2009. "The Construction of Space in Comics." In *A Comics Studies Reader*, edited by Jeet Heer and Kent Worcester, 157–62. Jackson: University Press of Mississippi.

Levitin, Daniel. 2006. *This Is Your Brain on Music: The Science of a Human Obsession*. New York: Plume.

Marx, Karl. 1977. "Private Property and Communism." *Economic and Philosophical Manuscripts of 1844.* In *Karl Marx: Selected Writings*, edited by David McLellan, 87–96. Oxford: Oxford University Press.

Merrifield, Andy. 2002. *Metromarxism: A Marxist Tale of the City.* New York: Routledge.

Mikkonen, Kai. 2017. *The Narratology of Comic Art.* New York: Routledge.

Molotiu, Andrei. 2012. "Abstract Form: Sequential Dynamism and Iconostasis in Abstract Comics and Steve Ditko's *Amazing Spider-Man.*" In *Critical Approaches to Comics: Theories and Methods*, edited by Matthew J. Smith and Randy Duncan, 84–100. New York: Routledge.

Moore, Alan W. 2004. "Political Economy as Subject and Form in Contemporary Art." *Review of Radical Political Economics* 36 (4): 471–86.

Murphy, Susan. 2002. "The Ordinary Street, the Storehouse of Treasures." In *Seeking the Centre: 2001 Australian International Religion, Literature and the Arts Conference Proceedings*, edited by Colette Rayment and Mark Levon Byrne, 154–68. Sydney: RLA Press.

Nadel, Dan, ed. 2021. *It's Life as I See It: Black Cartoonists in Chicago, 1940–1980.* New York: New York Review Comics / Museum of Contemporary Art Chicago.

Ogren, Brian. 2021. *Kabbalah and the Founding of America: The Early Influence of Jewish Thought in the New World.* New York: New York University Press.

Op de Beeck, Nathalie. 2006. "Found Objects: (Jem Cohen, Ben Katchor, Walter Benjamin)." *Modern Fiction Studies* 52 (4): 807–30.

Polland, Annie, and Daniel Soyer. 2012. *Emerging Metropolis: New York Jews in the Age of Immigration, 1840–1920.* Vol. 2 of *City of Promises: A History of the Jews of New York.* Foreword by Deborah Dash Moore. Visual essay by Diana L. Linden. New York: New York University Press.

Portnoy, Edward. 2008. "The Creation of a Jewish Cartoon Space in the New York and Warsaw Yiddish Press, 1884–1939." PhD diss., Jewish Theological Seminary of America.

Sacks, Oliver. 2007. *Musicophilia: Tales of Music and the Brain.* New York: Knopf.

Scholem, Gershom. 2015 [1960]. *Jewish Gnosticism, Merkabah Mysticism, and Talmudic Tradition.* New York: Jewish Theological Seminary of America.

Scholem, Gershom. 1995 [1941]. *Major Trends in Jewish Mysticism.* New York: Schocken Books.

Simmel, Georg. 2010 [1903]. "The Metropolis and Mental Life." In *The Blackwell City Reader*, 2nd ed., edited by Gary Bridge and Sophie Watson, 103–10. Malden, Oxford, and Chichester, UK: Wiley-Blackwell.

Van der Hoorn, Mélanie. 2012. *Bricks and Balloons: Architecture in Comic-Strip Form.* Rotterdam: 010 Publishers.

Weschler, Lawrence. 1993. "A Wanderer in the Perfect City." *New Yorker*, August 9, 1993, 58–67.

INDEX

Adorno, Theodor, viii–ix
architecture, 29, 51, 96; and comics
    form, 20, 26; pass-through, 42, 44;
    as psychological subspecialty, 58;
    and "victims of design," 6, 45, 110

books. *See* print culture

comics artists: Charles Johnson, 115n1;
    Chris Ware, 47, 117n27; Marc-
    Antoine Matthieu, 117n29; Richard
    F. Outcault, 101; Will Eisner, 117n27;
    Zuni Maud, 100
comics form: color in, 44, 59, 79–82; lay-
    out, 107; narration, 5, 18, 36, 94, 112;
    page fold, 27; paratextual elements,
    72, 84–88, 100; reading paths, 13;
    side-by-side strips, 20; word balloon
    stems, 38. *See also* time
comics scholars: Andrei Molotiu,
    117n28; Edward Portnoy, 121n9; Ian
    Hague, 9–10, 71–72, 117n24, 118n4,
    119n1; Kai Mikkonen, 118n16;
    Melanie Van de Horne, 117n27;
    Pascal Lefèvre, 118n15, 118n18;
    Thierry Groensteen, 112, 117n25,
    118n16. *See also* Katchor, Ben,
    scholarship on
commerce, 7, 28–29, 46; inventors,
    31, 46, 93–95; market economy,
    31, 74, 90, 93; object world, 34;

raw materials, 47, 62, 71, 84; and
    religion, 98–99; scarcity, 62; urban
    networks, 12
commune, 41, 64, 91
Communism, 31, 42
consumerism, 28–29, 32, 44, 46, 48, 58,
    63, 110

digital culture, 47, 71, 78

food, 8, 98, 104; and authenticity,
    105–6; canned, 105–10; cherry farm,
    52; eastern European, 64; Etruscan
    restaurant, 42; hunger, 50, 57;
    milk-based dining, 8, 99–100; room
    service, 47–48; sandwiches, 5, 56;
    soda, 28, 91, 99; vegetarianism, 8,
    100; viniculture, 53

hearing. *See* sound
humor, 32, 33; dark, 5; and debasement,
    59, 68; gags, 31, 100; and tragedy,
    6, 104

Judaism, 98–100, 112; Abraham
    Abulafia, 65–68; eastern European,
    ix, 7, 9, 101, 112; Gershom Scholem,
    118n6, 119n10; Hebrew, 63–65;
    Kabbalah, 54, 63, 65–70, 112; migra-
    tion, 101; Mordecai Manuel Noah,
    4; pogroms, 101; secular, 8–9, 92;

ABOUT THE AUTHOR

Photo by Abby Fuoto

Benjamin Fraser is professor in the College of Humanities at the University of Arizona. A scholar of comics and the urban experience, his previous books include the Eisner-nominated *The Art of Pere Joan: Space, Landscape, and Comics Form* (University of Texas Press, 2019); *Visible Cities, Global Comics: Urban Images and Spatial Form* (University Press of Mississippi, 2019); and *Barcelona, City of Comics* (State University of New York Press, 2022). His comics scholarship has appeared in the journals *European Comic Art, International Journal of Comic Art, Journal of Graphic Novels and Comics, ImageText: Interdisciplinary Comics Studies, Studies in Comics, Romance Studies, Transmodernity*, the *Bulletin of Spanish Visual Studies*, the *Journal of Spanish Cultural Studies*, and the edited volume *Spanish Comics* (2021, edited by Anne Magnussen). He is the founding editor of the *Journal of Urban Cultural Studies* and serves on the editorial board of *Studies in Comics*.